Warring at the Window

Window

Praying to Win

By Sharon Riddle

Every battle you will face can be won on your knees. If while reading this book you find the equipment or hope to face yours, lay the book down and wage war. Even if you never finish the book, I will be encouraged that it got you onto the field where victory can be won.

Olive Leaf Publications

To Uncle Dick
& Aunt Dorothy,
Thank you for
being such an integral
part of this project.
you both so much!

Acknowledgements

Thank you, Sally, for the editing and encouragement. (The Lord prepared her to help with the editing of this book through the training she received to become a medical transcriptionist.)

Thank you, Uncle Dick, Jean, Lowell and Terry, for returning my emails with suggestions. You knew what you were in for this time around and you still agreed to help. Smile. Your ideas were excellent and helped communicate the message so much more effectively.

Thank you, Sherry, Gary, Katherine and John, for allowing us to be refreshed in your corner of heaven (Jackson Hole, Wyoming) while the final edits were being done.

Thank you to my heroes: the men and women who labor daily alongside us in intercession. It is your sacrifices that have accomplished so much. You know who you are. Smile.

Contents

Introduction

The Lord is mustering the army for battle. Isaiah 13:4b

It was a beautiful, sunny day in the mountains of Yucaipa, California during the seventies. The youth of our denomination were gathering for a day of fun and spiritual encouragement. The event was called "The Armpit Olympics." In this event, teams with deodorant brand names like Arrid and Ban pitted themselves against each other. The highlight of the day was the tug of war over an oozing mud pit. I had forgotten about that in the morning as I dressed. I had worn a brand new pair of sunny, yellow shorts. Now as my team was called on to line up on one side of the great mud pit, I began to be concerned. Being dragged through the mud would be bad enough, but to ruin my brand new shorts would be unthinkable! The teams were in place and the whistle blew. It was easy to tell within a few seconds that my team was surely going to end up at the bottom of that mud pit. We were losing ground slowly, but surely. And then suddenly the thought of dull, gray shorts spurred me to action. I began yelling, "PULL!" with all my might. I don't know to this day why I did it. Something had risen up within me that said, "That's all I'm going to take!"

Then something miraculous began to happen. In rhythm to my cries my team began to pull. It wasn't my strength that turned the tide, but the strength of others that was put into action by my cries for help. Slowly my team began to back up with new strength. The other team was quickly being yanked from their stronghold. We now had the advantage and within seconds the battle was won.

That night at an awards ceremony, I was handed a spark plug in fun and told I was the spark plug to victory. The event left an impression because I realized that the only thing I had brought to my team was hope. It was a small offering, yet it helped win the battle.

Later on, as a pastor's wife, I recalled this incident while I watched the enemy drag families and ministries into his slimy pit of despair. As the Lord began to teach me more about prayer, I realized that my cries for help were all that was needed to put into motion the power of Another. Even when situations looked hopeless and lives were being tugged towards destruction, my cries for help to God could put into motion His strength and power. I might not have adequate wisdom, resources or strength to pull them out, but One was on the rope who could. My prayers were only an invitation for Him to participate.

Do you see our world being slowly pulled deeper and deeper into trouble? Do you want to do something about it? Do you see family members and friends having their lives pulled out from under them by a crafty enemy who wants to destroy them? Do you want to see Satan's plans end up in the mud pit? If so, then this book is for you. The Lord has packed His Word with power. The purpose of this book is to teach you skills in warfare so that ammunition can be stockpiled, weapons sharpened, and lives saved. The battle rages on around us. Let's meet at the window of prayer ready for war.

Who is the King of glory? The Lord strong and mighty. The Lord mighty in battle. Psalm 24:8

The Lord will go forth like a warrior, He will arouse His zeal like a man of war. He will utter a shout, yes, He will raise a war cry. He will prevail against His enemies. Isaiah 42:13

If you're not a prayer warrior, you'll be a casualty!

They have blown the trumpet and made everything ready, but no one is going to the battle. Ezekiel 7:14a

How have the mighty fallen, and the weapons of war perished! 2 Samuel 1:27

"I'm not a prayer warrior," a friend said to me recently. "I'll just tell my wife to pray about it." This was his response to a request for prayer that I had shared with him. Could this have been your part of a conversation? To say you're not a prayer warrior doesn't mean you don't live in a war zone. Your mental rejection of participation does not somehow protect you from the arrows being flung by the minute.

It simply says that you have resigned yourself to being one of the casualties.

All around you, the enemy hurls his weapons, takes captives and enjoys the booty that is legally yours. But as long as you live in denial, rejecting the use of the weapons that have been entrusted to you, you will be defeated in the onslaught. It just means that you have chosen to do nothing more than become a walking target for his schemes.

If you choose to go deeper in prayer, you will be able to repel the deadly lies that the devil has chosen to blind you. Your whispered hopes and dreams will become a catapult that returns fire to the enemy and releases captives held in his grasp.

God is no respecter of persons. He answers every cry for help. He listens to every uttered prayer. He even hears prayers with no words, only sighs and groans. If you are not a prayer warrior, it is not because you don't possess the potential to become one. It is because you are choosing not to participate in God's offensive strategy.

Today, make a decision to take up the sword you already possess. Utter prayers that hinder the enemy's plans. Even a child can do it! The Almighty One can use any desires you can voice. The Holy Spirit is always available to interpret our hopes in the light of His will. (*And He who searches the hearts knows what the mind of the Spirit is, because He intercedes for the saints according to the will of God. Romans 8:27*) Don't worry that you can't see the enemy's schemes, only the path of destruction he leaves in his wake. Your prayers will hit the heart of his efforts every time because the Lord God directs their flight.

Line up the shield and buckler, and draw near for the battle! Harness the horses, and mount the steeds, and take your stand with helmets on! Polish the spears, put on the scale-armor! Jeremiah 46:3-4
But in everything commending ourselves as servants of God, in much endurance, in afflictions, in hardships, in distresses... in the word of truth, in the power of God; by the weapons of righteousness for the right hand and the left... 2 Corinthians 6:4a, 7

Chapter 1 - Don't be the Enemy's Tool

They band themselves together against the life of the righteous, and condemn the innocent to death. Psalm 94:21

A heavenly view of a spiritual encounter

Have you ever wondered what our spiritual battles look like from God's perspective? Have you ever considered what is going on in the mind of Satan as he studies the entries next to your name in his daily planner? In 1 Chronicles chapter twenty-one we get to view a spiritual encounter in David's life that can give us insight into the methods and motives of our enemy, while helping us to incorporate tools for the destruction of his strategies. Take a few minutes to read this passage in your Bible and then let's begin to look deeply into its truths.

The first thing we notice in this passage is that Satan intentionally moves to inflict harm on God's people. He's not a nice guy who's been saddled with a bad reputation. He's a destroyer to the core.

The devil and his demons get up each day seeking to strike out at God through His people. In this instance, Satan purposefully chose Israel as a target. (*1 Chronicles 21:1 Then Satan stood up against Israel and moved David to number Israel.*) You can almost picture Satan standing by a world map with a pointer in his hand. He is choosing a target for destruction. Does he pick a country that worships idols? Does he select a nation entrenched in demon worship? No, he picks out a country that represents the heart of God. He chooses a nation that lives by God's principles.

And so it is that America has become Satan's target. Because we have for so long represented Judeo-Christian principles in government and have been a godly nation (although you could hardly call us that now), we have become the nation circled on Satan's strategic map.

A friend of mine, who prays regularly at an abortion clinic with me, said something wise to me one day: "If nobody's shootin' at you,

you're probably on the wrong side of the street." If you are attempting to do what is right in this world, you can just bet that your chest has a great big bulls-eye on it. You are a target for the enemy. One of my favorite *Far Side* cartoons depicts two deer. One has a target on his chest. The other, reflecting on it says to him: "Bummer of a birth mark!" Yet those of us who have been birthed into the family of God also bear a similar mark. We have become the objects of Satan's demoralizing plots. The birthmark is for life. The good news is that God has put His mark on us also.

The posture of warfare

Isn't it interesting that we see the physical posture of Satan change as he approaches this encounter? Scripture says, "Satan stood up against Israel." It's like he's reclining and then all of a sudden he stands up, ready to go to war. So doesn't it make sense that when we fight him, we take a stand also? We can be in a resting mode or a fighting mode, but not both at the same time. We are told many times in Scripture to "take your stand." When we can't do anything else, we are encouraged to stand. Our posture denotes our purpose. We get up when we have had enough from Satan and are ready to act. Look around our world. Have you had enough? Start standing up to the enemy's work.

Be on the alert, stand firm in the faith, act like men, be strong. 1 Corinthians 16:13

Satan is purpose driven

Satan's attacks are aimed at one thing: he wants to leave God's people dead as food for the birds. (Psalm 79:2.) His attacks are not random or without thought. When we read Psalm 83:3-5 we get a view into the mind of our enemy: *They make shrewd plans against Thy people, and conspire together against Thy treasured ones. They have said, "Come, and let us wipe them out as a nation, that the name of Israel be remembered no more." For they have conspired together with one mind; against Thee do they make a covenant."* Psalm 17:11 tells us: *They have surrounded us in their steps; they set their eyes to cast us down to the ground.* He and his demons have one goal. They don't squabble about what they are trying to accomplish. They are in constant agreement. As our friend Dr. Rick Warren would note, they are "purpose-driven" in their efforts. They want you put out of commission. They aren't going to get distracted with what color carpet you'll die on. They aren't going to use up valuable energy fighting about who gets to be on the committee or who gets the credit. They are all willing to work together with one mind to see the job to victory.

So why is it that when we fight against Satan, we don't use the same strategy? We are at our best when we are one. That's why Jesus prayed for unity for His church, His bride (John 17:11). He knew that of all the tactics we have to fight the enemy, one of the most powerful ones we can employ is being of one mind. We must constantly keep this in mind. Satan's goal is to divide us as God's people. Our power comes from being one church empowered by one God. We need not only to take a stand; we need to do it together.

For one warrior has stumbled over another, and both of them have fallen down together. Jeremiah 46:12b

Two are better than one because they have a good return for their labor. For if either of them falls, the one will lift up his companion. But woe to the one who falls when there is not another to lift him up. And if one can overpower him who is alone, two can resist him. A cord of three strands is not quickly torn apart. Ecclesiastes 4:9-10,12

You might agree on ninety-nine things with another Christian brother or sister, but when the enemy goes to work, you better believe that he will do his best to focus the spotlight on the one thing on which you disagree. Beware when you see a relationship that has been strong and sure for years getting pounded by misunderstanding and grief. Realize what the devil is trying to do and resist his efforts. Focus on the things that unite. Focus on the big picture. Focus on things that last. When at war with Iraq, the soldiers didn't squabble in the foxholes over who was a Democrat or a Republican. No, they focused on something worth being united over: ending terrorism.

One of the devil's most effective weapons over the course of history has been division. It isolates, it diminishes resources and it weakens the effectiveness of our prayers. All of these things are accomplished when we act as individuals and not in corporate oneness.

Note: those who move into the realm of deeper prayer should constantly be on the alert for the devil's subtle plants of untruth about their prayer partners. He often tries to get prayer warriors to doubt each other's integrity or methods. Why? So they will stop praying together.

He is like a lion that is eager to tear, and as a young lion lurking in hiding places. Psalm 17:12

Thought: the devil never takes a vacation! (I discovered this when we returned from vacation one year to a pile of trouble.)

One of the greatest tools, then, in spiritual warfare, is a spirit of unity. The more we agree together, the more power and influence we have over our enemy. When we pray at an abortion clinic, we are joined by our Catholic friends. Over the past years we have seen the Lord developing a close camaraderie between us. He has been slowly breaking down the barriers that Satan has so craftily constructed. The result has been more power and effectiveness in our prayers.

Then Satan stood up against Israel and moved David to number Israel. 1 Chronicles 21:1

Scripture describes Satan choosing a tool for this daily assignment. He picks of all people, David, God's anointed servant. At the beginning of this chapter we see that David is spiritually unprepared for battle. Satan is standing up, but David is sitting down. David's in the middle of a spiritual encounter and he's counting nickels and noses, not interceding for his people. He's spouting his strength. He's a one-man-show. He's prayerless and prideful. He is complacent, even cocky. He's evaluating his glory.

In contrast, the David we read about at the end of this chapter is on his face before God. He's in worship with the elders of Israel. He is aware of his weakness. He discovers how wretched he is. The discovery qualifies him to be the right one to be king after all.

And lest you think that you are above being Satan's instrument, "take heed, lest you fall." Any one of us can be an instrument of destruction in the hands of the enemy. All it takes is a little resting, a little folding of the hands, a little sitting down on the job of interceding, and we become a prime candidate for trouble. Here is David, a man with a heart for God, who stirred up the trouble. It is true that those who are greatly used by God can also cause the greatest harm.

For example, it is the devil who encourages Peter to spout the words "May it never be!" in connection with Christ setting His course for the cross. Thank goodness the Lord identifies the source of that thought for those who lack spiritual discernment. "Get thee behind me Satan!" is His response. We thought it was Peter who was talking, but no, it was the enemy trying to use Peter as a tool to discourage the Son of God from obedience. Jesus also identifies the spiritual state that made Peter vulnerable to the enemy's influence: Matthew 16:23 But He turned and said to Peter, "Get behind Me, Satan! You (to Peter) are a stumbling block to Me; for you are not setting your mind on God's interests, but man's." Luke 6:45b tells us that the mouth speaks from that which fills his heart. We must therefore, give constant attention to our thought life and to our affections if we are to avoid Satan's tricks. He wants to use us to discourage others. An angry reaction, a harmful word, or a distraction from God's purpose is what he wants. Leave Satan empty-handed today. Choose to set your mind and heart on the will of God.

When a humble pastor, who loves God and has been greatly used by Him sins, many people are affected. When an elder who appears to have a faithful life is found faithless, it causes many to stumble. Satan is roaming to and fro, looking for someone to devour. Don't let it be you. Try to see everything through eternity's filter.

I can get my feathers ruffled so easily. If something isn't going like I think it should, I can get my nose out of joint and cause more harm than good. In the middle of conflict I try to ask myself: "Will this issue matter when I stand before Jesus?" If not, it's probably just a ploy of the enemy to bring down the strategic defense of unity. Ask yourself in the midst of every spiritual battle: in this situation, am I Satan's target, or his tool? One thing is for sure, I don't want to be useful to the enemy.

The most dangerous Christian is one who is out of fellowship with Jesus, so a first defense in warfare is to be constantly devoted to a right relationship with God and man (communion), to the study of God's Word, to prayer and to fellowship, the earmarks of the New Testament church. *And they were continually devoting themselves to the apostles' teaching and to fellowship, to the breaking of bread and to prayer. Acts 2:42*

Then Satan stood up against Israel and moved David to number Israel. 1 Chronicles 21:1

Then the enemy walks over to his pile of tried-and-true methods and picks up the method of choice for this encounter. On this particular day he selected "numbering" as his weapon. It doesn't seem like that big of a sin to take a census of Israel. But when you've lived a life of trust, one baby step of calculating man's resources versus God's provision is a huge stumble. Like a tightrope walker who must keep his eyes focused on the goal, not the ground, so a follower of God must keep his eyes focused on the Resource Giver, not the resource itself. Satan's goal is not to get you onto a different road all at once. He just wants you off course a few degrees. It doesn't matter in the end how far he got you off course, just that he did get you redirected. So it is with the spiritual leaders of today. Numbering the followers is a source of feeding the fleshly desire for fame.

Even blessings can be distractions. A friend of mine shared recently that when she and her husband were financially strapped, they had to depend on the Lord daily for every need. But when the blessings of their obedience began to come, they found they were in a spiritual "slump." Their need had kept them close. Their abundance became a distraction. And so it was with David. The very thing that was God's blessing, a huge army, had gotten his eyes off the goal and onto himself. The man, who had been protected by the power of God as he hid in caves from his enemy Saul, had now become vulnerable to the enemy by an interesting method: the blessings of power and influence.

Instruct those who are rich in this present world not to be conceited or to fix their hope on the uncertainty of riches, but on God, who richly supplies us with all things to enjoy. Instruct them to do good, to be rich in good works, to be generous and ready to share, storing up for themselves the treasure of a good foundation for the future, so that they may take hold of that which is life indeed. 1 Timothy 6:17-19

Note: This is indeed the strategy we need to learn to be victorious in times of blessing. Focus on the Giver of the gifts. Recognize that when God gives good gifts, it is because He wants us to enjoy them. God's gifts should result in good deeds done by us to others. If we are being blessed and others are not being affected by a generous heart, there is a problem that must be addressed and confessed. We must keep eternity in our thinking at all times. Money is transient, but blessings are eternal. This is God's truth about real living.

I was reading the words to the hymn "In the Garden" the other day, and one little phrase caught my attention: "But He bids me go, through a world of woe..." It's trouble that drives us to the feet of Jesus. But we hate it so. We long for abundance and peace, but unfortunately, it is hard to live this way without putting our feet up, taking a rest, and getting into trouble. This is the very thing that happened to David. We read earlier that when the other kings went out to battle, he stayed home. In the end he sinned with Bathsheba because he was at rest when he should have been at war. He was lying down when he should have been standing up.

Again, in this incident, we see a careless, relaxed David. He was the most likely target because he was such an unlikely suspect. Why would anyone be on their guard against a devoted worshipper of God? That is why this method of the enemy is so effective. We are taken by surprise every time.

The method doesn't really matter to Satan. He will use any course that works. He learns what works through watching you react. He's not omniscient. He gains knowledge through experience, and so as he observes your life, he can see patterns develop. He knows what you like by watching what you go after. Remember in the book <u>The Lion, Witch and the Wardrobe</u>, by C.S. Lewis that the temptation offered by the Wicked Witch to one of the children was called Turkish Delight? Turkish Delight is a great term that describes whatever you desire. God promises to fulfill our needs and our dreams in His time, but Satan offers them up front, with no waiting. He offered dominion to Jesus, who would rightfully gain it in the end according to the Father's plan, not Satan's plan. He offered the wisdom of God to Eve, who already had it right in her own back yard. He offers what he knows you want.

Remember David wasn't always a powerful king. He was the youngest brother who was ridiculed and put down prior to his encounter with Goliath. (*Now Eliab his oldest brother heard when he spoke to the men; and Eliab's anger burned against David and he said, "Why have you come down? And with whom have you left those few sheep in the wilderness? I know your insolence and the wickedness of your heart; for you have come down in order to see the battle."* *1 Samuel 17:28*) He was an inexperienced soldier in untried armor. (*David girded his sword over his armor and tried to walk, for he had not tested them. So David said to Saul, "I cannot go with these, for I have not tested them." And David took them off. 1 Samuel 17:39*) He was a kingly candidate who was harassed and persecuted. (*Then David arose and fled that day from Saul, and went to Achish king of Gath. But the servants of Achish said to him, "Is this not David the king of the land? Did they not sing of this one as they danced, saying, 'Saul has slain his thousands, and David his ten thousands'?" 1 Samuel 21:10-11*)

8

David keenly desired the honor and respect of others. God had a plan to give him this, but Satan wanted him to jump into the express line. If you have a big army, then you are a big man. And so it goes; Satan holds out a plate of Turkish Delight (just our flavor) and waits to see if we will shortchange God's future blessing for the pleasure of immediate satisfaction.

Now look with me at another aspect of this encounter: God's view of the situation. At the same time we see Satan "get up" to cause trouble, we see something else. We see the omnipotent God who can take anything the devil dishes out and turn the tables with it. No matter what strategy the enemy engages, God is able to "turn it for good" in the lives of His people. (*And we know that God causes all things to work together for good to those who love God, to those who are called according to His purpose. Romans 8:28*) It's so great to be on the Lord's side. When we obey, there's always victory! Satan might shovel out abuse, heartache and despair but God answers back, "I can use that!"

So David said to Joab and to the princes of the people, "Go, number Israel from Beersheba even to Dan, and bring me word that I may know their number." And Joab said, "May the Lord add to His people a hundred times as many as they are! But, my lord the king, are they not all my lord's servants? Why does my lord seek this thing? Why should he be a cause of guilt to Israel?" 1 Chronicles 21:2-3

God promises in 1 Corinthians 10:13, that in every spiritual encounter He will provide a door of escape. Here he does it through a trusted friend. Because God loved David and Israel, out of compassion, He sent someone to "check" David's thinking. Not many will question a king, but Joab got right to the heart of the issue. Why do you want this thing? What personal need is the motivation for numbering Israel? Sometimes we are David (the one needing a rebuke) and sometimes we are Joab (asking why are you so set on doing this—what's at the heart of this decision?). Joab was trying to help David see the giant of self that was interfering with the job of governing his country.

9

"Are they not all my lord's servants?" 1 Chronicles 21:3—selected

Joab reminds David of truth: "Isn't everybody in Israel your servant?" As friends involved every day in spiritual conflict, one of the best things we can do for each other is remind each other of the truth. We find it all through His Word. When friends are struggling we can point them to hope. When they are weary, we can point them to God's strength. Out of a heart of love, we just point to the truth.

One of the Bible study teachers at our church tells our women to "pull out their trump cards" when the enemy comes calling. These are just 3x5 cards with verses written on them. "Just remember that a trump card presides over any other card that gets played," she says. And in the same way, the truth of God's Word will always be victorious over circumstances. Job 42:2b tells us that *"no purpose of Thine can be thwarted"* and Isaiah 8:10 reminds us: *"Devise a plan but it will be thwarted; state a proposal, but it will not stand, for God is with us."* When Satan deals you a losing set of circumstances, play your trump cards. Remind him of the truth of God's Word.

Why should he be a cause of guilt to Israel? 1 Chronicles 21:3b

God was faithful to send a rebuke through a friend to the stubborn-hearted king. *Faithful are the wounds of a friend, but deceitful are the kisses of an enemy. Proverbs 27:6* Here we see Joab being a real friend to David. Sometimes the best thing to share in spiritual conflict is the hardest thing to say. There are people all around you who are making foolish decisions, but you don't have to just let them follow through. You can risk rejection by saying, "Hey, you're going to ruin your life if you leave your wife." "Don't throw away the precious gift of your child by being stubborn in this situation." "Stop throwing your life away and start fulfilling the great calling God has placed on your life."

But he did not number Levi and Benjamin among them, for the king's command was abhorrent to Joab. 1 Chronicles 21:6

Even Joab, who did not always make wise decisions, can see that this course of action is wrong. Why can't David see it? He is suffering from temporary insanity. (Like someone caught up in infatuation, he is not making good decisions.) That is why we are encouraged in the New Testament to keep our eyesight clear through right relationship with God. There will be times when our brother or sister has some spiritual visual impediment. We need each other at those times to get out the magnifying mirror of God's Word and dislodge the impediment that blinds us. I am glad that Joab did not number the Levites or the tribe of Benjamin. Perhaps the lives of the priests were spared from the death that occurred to seventy thousand other men that day!

And why do you look at the speck that is in your brother's eye, but do not notice the log that is in your own eye? Or how can you say to your brother, "Let me take the speck out of your eye," and behold, the log is in your own eye? You hypocrite, first take the log out of your own eye, and then you will see clearly to take the speck out of your brother's eye. Matthew 7:3-5

Nevertheless, the king's word prevailed against Joab. Therefore, Joab departed and went throughout all Israel, and came to Jerusalem. 1 Chronicles 21:4

Sometimes our sin is our lack of intercession. Samuel says: *"...far be it from me to sin by ceasing to pray for you." 1 Samuel 12:23* Sometimes our problem is the bad thing we do and sometimes it is just the good thing we fail to do. When we take a good look at the Epistles, we see this constant intercession exemplified in the life of Paul. Paul tells the churches under his care that he's always praying for them—night and day. How can we expect to be victorious in spiritual warfare if we are not doing the same? We are told in Luke 22:40b: *"Pray that you may not enter into temptation."* There is a definite connection between the heart that is in prayer and the one who enjoys victory over sin. So move on in prayer that you might become a conqueror over sin.

And God was displeased with this thing, so He struck Israel. 1 Chronicles 21:7

Sometimes you learn more through the things you lose, than through the things you win. Seventy thousand men lost their lives, but a leader became a man after God's heart. The realization was costly, but worthwhile. In a similar way, the Apostle Paul had to sit across from the family members of the Christians he had slain while yet a "pre-Christian." Everyday he had to look his sin in the face as he taught the relatives of those he had ordered to death. But when we hear him admit that he is the chief of all sinners, we know that the cost has been worth it. A man who realizes his utter dependence on the righteousness of Jesus Christ is one who can be useful. Many gave their lives so the apostle Paul could learn this valuable lesson, but once learned many others found true life through his example. Whose suffering and sacrifice paved the way for the spiritual maturity and growth you are experiencing today? For a true shepherd, any sacrifice is worthwhile if it moves a heart closer to the Lord.

We have seen many come to know the Lord throughout our ministry, but it never ceases to delight my heart to see fully devoted servants where an unbeliever once stood. When our church was so little that there was only one service with barely seventy in attendance, we faced a problem: we couldn't get enough nursery workers. Now this is a challenge that many churches face, big or small, but this time God chose to use a problem to give us a long-term blessing. Those who served in the nursery had to miss church and this was a deterrent to serving. Add to that the fact that many in our church were young Christians and you will understand that we faced a crisis. So we chose a course of action that in retrospect doesn't look like such a good idea: we hired an unbeliever. Yvonne was the neighbor of someone in our church. She was good with children and needed a job. We hired her and she began doing a great job. (I am not recommending what we did, just what God did in spite of it. Smile.)

It wasn't long after this that Yvonne approached me with a question, "Could I serve every other week?" I wasn't too thrilled to hear the question, but I was thrilled with the motivation. Yvonne wanted to work every other week so she could start attending church! Shortly after this she gave her heart to the Lord, as did her live-in boyfriend, Jeff. The Holy Spirit convicted them to get married and they began growing by leaps and bounds.

Eventually, they began serving in others areas, teaching and leading. Then a few years later they moved out of state. Recently I got to speak to the women of Yvonne's church in Washington where she is a leader. How I thank the Lord for the many changes He has brought about in their family, all are saved and are serving the Lord, and their extended family (Yvonne's mother and two brothers have become Christians). All the sacrifices we made in the early years of ministry fade into nothing in comparison to victories like these. Praise the Lord!

How much suffering will result from your sin today? Who will be disheartened when you stay home from church? How many will not get the nourishment they need because you are disobedient about your ministry?

Do you remember the game of Red Rover? If you were the adversary, then you looked for the frailest little kid to charge over. It's the same with Satan. He looks down the row of Christians and picks out those who are weak in prayer as future targets. Don't end up being his choice. Don't be a weak link in the chain. Enter the gym of deeper prayer and bulk up.

And David said to God, "I have sinned greatly, in that I have done this thing. But now, please take away the iniquity of Thy servant, for I have done very foolishly." And David said to God, "Is it not I who commanded to count the people? Indeed, I am the one who has sinned and done very wickedly, but these sheep, what have they done? O Lord my God, please let Thy hand be against me and my father's household, but not against Thy people that they should be plagued."
1 Chronicles 21:8, 17

The marvelous thing about this spiritual warfare encounter is that eventually David recognized his own sin. When we can see our sin, we can confess it. When we confess sin, it can be cleansed and removed. The whole crux is seeing the problem. We can be the problem in spiritual warfare. We can be complacent and blind. We can be counting noses while our world is headed for destruction. But seeing the problem is the beginning of the solution.

Let's begin our quiet time today with this realization: "Lord, let me see my sin. Let me understand the havoc that has been wreaked on my world through my lack of intercession." Once we acknowledge it, and repent of it, it can be removed forever.

And David said to Gad, "I am in great distress; please let me fall into the hand of the Lord, for His mercies are very great. But do not let me fall into the hand of man." 1 Chronicles 21:13

David knew that the character of God was woven with mercy. He counted on it. You and I worship the same God. God can no more give up His mercy than He can His power or wisdom. You can count on it. You can take it to the bank. When you see your sin and truly repent of it, you can know that you'll find forgiveness waiting for you.

Then David lifted up his eyes and saw the angel of the Lord standing between earth and heaven, with his drawn sword in his hand stretched out over Jerusalem. Then David and the elders, covered with sackcloth, fell on their faces. 1 Chronicles 21:16

Not only did David see his sin, but he saw God in a new way. Many things come into perspective when we really see God. Like Isaiah, who was sent out to do good, like Moses, who encountered a fiery version of the presence of God in a bush, when we get into the real presence of God and experience His fullness, then our circumstances shrink in the light of His magnificence. You can't view the awesome greatness of God and shrink in fear of the enemy. God towers over Satan's puniness. Therefore, one of the greatest tools in spiritual combat that we can ever understand is the powerful presence of the Most High God.

The Lord is faithful, who will establish you and guard you from the evil one. 2 Thessalonians 3:3 NKJ

Now to Him who is able to keep you from stumbling, and to present you faultless before the presence of His glory with exceeding joy; to God our Savior, who alone is wise, be glory and majesty, dominion and power, both now and forever. Jude 24-25 NKV

The glimpse David got of God was profound. God's sword was drawn over the city of Jerusalem. This is the picture of God we need to hold onto in difficult situations. God is not pacing back and forth over a dwindling supply depot. He is not wringing His hands over the wounded. He is a warrior in the trenches, protecting His own people. He is drawing the line around them and their resources. He is fighting for us. Therefore our prayers are not His wake up call. They are our wake up call. We are not pricking Him to stand up and fight. They are pricking us to line up with His will in the battle.

Hence, also, He is able to save forever those who draw near to God through Him, since He always lives to make intercession for them. Hebrews 7:25

Because David saw more about God than he had ever seen before, his worship was bumped up to a new level. The worship service we read about in I Chronicles 21:21-30 is the best part of the whole story.

But King David said to Ornan, "No, but I will surely buy it for the full price; for I will not take what is yours for the Lord, or offer a burnt offering which costs me nothing." 1 Chronicles 21:24

Because David gets an idea of how awful his sin was, he came before God with a truly honest heart (repentant and ready to admit neediness). God in turn revealed more of who He really was. He is a

God of compassion and mercy, so David found ready forgiveness. Therefore, now David was praying in right relationship with God. There were consequences for his sin, but God was committed to using the incident for good. Ornan wanted to treat him to the privileges of a king, but David suddenly saw the joy in being a servant. He was no longer hungering for honor, but for service. He was at a place to really meet God. He wanted to give from a whole heart (like Barnabas who wanted to give his field in Acts 4:36-37).

Then David built an altar to the Lord there, and offered burnt offerings and peace offerings. And he called to the Lord and He answered him with fire from heaven on the altar of burnt offering. 1 Chronicles 21:26

Everything David and the nation of Israel had gone through was worth it at this point. God answered true worship with fire. The death of many became worthwhile to see the birth of this one new thing. Seventy thousand families lost loved ones, but David and the elders of Israel gained an intimacy with God. Every spiritual encounter you face that causes you to respond yes to God results in a new place with Him. You cannot be obedient and not be brought near. David's prayer life moved to a new level. He called to the Lord and the Lord answered.

What was the fire like that was God's response to David's prayer that day? I know from my own encounters with the living God that when I pray the right kind of prayer, from the right state of heart, there can be a responsive heart-fire from God. Like Bristlecone pinecones opened in a forest fire, the seeds of new dreams are opened from Heaven and begin to plant a forest of activity in our hearts.

Start today with an honest evaluation of the state of your intercession for others. Admit your sin and agree to meet God at the threshing floor of your home. Then look out! Because the place where you are standing is where the Captain of the Host of Heaven has taken His stand. His blazing sword is drawn, and your prayers will be the eye-salve that lets you experience fresh vision with Him.

Chapter 2 - Know the Living Word of God

...be it done to me according to Your Word... Luke 1:38b

God's Word contains all the direction we need for each day's circumstances

God's Word was God-breathed when it was written. Nothing has changed. It is still God-breathed. It is general. It is specific. God can direct me through it. If I am seeking His will with no unconfessed sin and if I am willing to wait for His marching orders, then I can seek God's voice through His Word to direct me in the way I should go. The same God, who aligned the universe in perfect order, is capable of directing me, His servant, through the course of the day. I have seen over and over again how God's Word is a true lamp unto my feet and a light unto my path.

When people are searching for the will of God in their lives, I want them to know this truth: they can come with honest hearts and find direction through the specific guidance of God's Word—that is to say, as much of God's will as He wants me to know at this moment in time. It is important to remember that the Bible is only one of the ways God directs us. He also uses godly council, experience, circumstances, the promptings of the Holy Spirit and dreams/visions/signs to show His people what His will is.

Some people misunderstand this principle. They randomly open their Bibles and play Bible Roulette. They read the first line their eyes focus on and take that to be God's answer to their dilemma (like an ouija board). That is not what I am referring to; what I do mean is that when we read God's Word consistently and completely, coupled with a prayer for direction, God uses it to guide our actions and refine our attitudes.

For example, I recently attended a gathering of Christian leaders where I was to sign copies of my first book. Unfortunately, the books were shipped too late to arrive for the convention. I knew two days before I left California that there would be no books to sign. But I had seen God's hand in preparing everything for this trip. First let me explain. Back in February of 2003 I had wanted to attend the convention, held in July of that same year, but at that time I didn't have a penny towards the expenses. This would be another chance to take an adventure of waiting on Jesus.

Month after month I continued to pray. Then in May I received the resources that indicated to me that I was to go. The Lord marvelously provided a large gift of money for our family, not earmarked for any other ministry venture, that could be used for the trip. However, when I called my contact person at the publisher, she let me know that all the "author spots" that their company had been given were taken. Money or no money, there was no space. I remember giving her a word of testimony that went something like this, "I'm not sure I understand this whole situation. Every day as I have brought it before the Lord, I have had the sense that the Lord has been encouraging me. When He provided all the money, I felt sure I was to go. So, don't be surprised if something opens up. Just call me, OK? I'll be ready." That was in April. It was in June that I got a call saying that someone who had planned to go could not come. I was asked, "Would you like to take his place?" I rejoiced in the God of details, who had taken care of everything. Not only had the fees been provided, but also my housing and airfare, even down to the clothing I would wear. It had all been provided.

But now, four days before I was to leave, I found out that the initial purpose I thought the trip was for, signing books, must not be what God had in mind. So I consulted His Word. God has a way of sticking post-it notes from His Word in my thoughts as I enjoy my daily quiet time. He illumines some verses more than others to help focus my mind on His desires.

One verse that I felt He had illuminated was this: *For you were called to freedom, brethren; only do not turn your freedom into an opportunity for the flesh, but through love serve one another. Galatians 5:13* I felt that the Lord was telling me through this verse that the trip had little to do with selling a lot of books, but instead, was an opportunity to serve others. Because I began the trip with the focus of service, I found plenty of opportunities to do just that. I got to help another author with her book signing. I was able to encourage a wayward Christian for several hours on one of the legs of my flight. I got to share enthusiasm, prayer and faith with another writer while we were promoting our books together. I taught some prayer lessons to specific individuals who asked genuine questions. I got to intercede for the Christian book industry with greater urgency and deeper understanding.

God's Word is the place for encouragement and hope

Each night as I arrived back in my hotel room, the discouragement of the flesh would attack. "Why am I even here? This is all a big waste of time and money," were some of the thoughts that crossed my mind. I had to get a new supply of hope for each day of the adventure, but I was never disappointed by the truths of God's Word. They, like God Himself, are full of hope. God's Word cannot discourage you. Each night I would plead with the Lord to give me marching orders for the next day and here are some of the verses God used to specifically guide me.

For God has power to help and to bring down. 2 Chronicles 25:8b

God promotes and demotes. His help is all that is needed to promote a book or any other project. Without Him, there is nothing one can do to move forward. This truth brought a joyful calm to my heart as I meditated on it. In the perspective of a year's time since the trip, we have seen that God has sold hundreds of copies of this book for His glory. Praise the Lord!

And Amaziah said to the man of God, "But what shall we do for the hundred talents which I have given to the troops of Israel?" And the man of God answered, "The Lord has much more to give you than this." 2 Chronicles 25:9

God used this verse to comfort me as I, like Amaziah, worried about the money I had spent on this trip that seemed wasted. In this passage Amaziah has hired soldiers from Israel to help him fight the battle and God tells him to send them home. God says "I am not with them." In other words, if you go ahead with this plan you'll lose, because I cannot bless those who choose sin. Amaziah's question is, "But what about the money I've spent?" God tells Him that he should not worry about it; that God can provide all he needs to do His will and more. I knew the Lord had directed me to be on this trip. Nevertheless, I still felt unsure about the resources I had spent. God assured my heart, through this verse, not to worry about it. Being in the center of His will was the important thing. It's easy to see now that the Lord has kept His promise to me. The year 2004 was the biggest year of financial blessing our family has ever experienced. Praise the Lord!

And he continued to seek God in the days of Zechariah, who had understanding through the vision of God; and as long as he sought the Lord, God prospered him. 2 Chronicles 26:5 And God helped him... 2 Chronicles 26:7a ... for he became very strong. 2 Chronicles 26:8b ... for he was marvelously helped until he was strong. 2 Chronicles 26:15b So Jotham became mighty because he ordered his ways before the Lord his God. 2 27:6 Then Hezekiah and all the people rejoiced over what God had prepared for the people, because the thing came about suddenly. 2 Chronicles 29:36

While at the convention I couldn't see all that God had prepared for future blessings. I simply had to concentrate on "ordering my ways before Him." But in response to my obedience, God blessed me with some incredible opportunities to share that I could have never gotten on my own. One day He suddenly opened the opportunity for me to speak about prayer and my first book on our local radio station every day for a week. Praise the Lord!

Then Hezekiah spoke encouragingly to all the Levites who showed good insight in the things of the Lord. 2 Chronicles 30:22a

Then the Levitical priests arose and blessed the people; and their voice was heard and their prayer came to His holy dwelling place, to heaven. 2 Chronicles 30:27

I interpreted these verses to mean that I was to speak words of encouragement when I saw things that warranted it: i.e., talking to the president of the Christian Booksellers Association and telling him how much I appreciated the emphasis on prayer. I focused on being an encourager to many of the ministries represented at the convention who had made an impact on my life. The convention was discouraging to many because of the slow economy, but in the midst of it, the Lord wanted me to generously dish out encouragement. He needed a servant, not a signer. As the week progressed I saw that the famine of spiritual depth throughout the industry. It has shown me how to pray for this vital key in the restoration of our country and this resource for revival.

"Be strong and courageous, do not fear or be dismayed because of the king of Assyria, nor because of all the multitude which is with him; for the one with us is greater than the one with him. With him is only an arm of flesh, but with us is the Lord our God to help us and to fight our battles." And the people relied on the words of Hezekiah king of Judah. 2 Chronicles 32:7-8

Thou hast enclosed me behind and before, and laid Thy hand upon me. Such knowledge is too wonderful for me; it is too high, I cannot attain to it. Psalm 139:5-6

To understand that God has His hand on us is a wonderful thought. How can the enemy stand against us when God's hand rests on us? Even though I am just one in a multitude, because God is with me, I have the advantage over those who do not.

The Lord will accomplish what concerns me; Psalm 138:8a Whatever the Lord pleases, He does, in heaven and in earth, in the seas and in all deeps. Psalm 135:6

The Lord is going to do what He wants to do. If He wants to sell a book, no one can stop Him. If He doesn't want it sold, all the publicity and money in the world won't do a bit of good.

For I know that this shall turn out for my deliverance through your prayers and the provision of the Spirit of Jesus Christ according to my earnest expectation and hope, that I shall not be put to shame in anything, but that with all boldness, Christ shall even now, as always, be exalted in my body, whether by life or by death. Philippians 1:19-20

I was constantly aware during this trip of the power of the prayers of others. In the most hopeless of circumstances, still I believed that I would not be ashamed of trusting God to use my life to give Him glory on this trip. When I returned from the trip, one of the elders at our church told me that he was very aware of the Lord pricking him to intercede for me. I told him, "Thank you, I really needed it!" I knew the battle that had gone on. This trip was an incredible spiritual victory I will never forget. God picked me to use for His purposes and I am so glad my friend prayed me through.

Let your forbearing spirit be known to all men. The Lord is near. Philippians 4:5 The king granted him all he requested because the hand of the Lord his God was upon him. Ezra 7:6b For the Lord will judge His people, and will have compassion on His servants. Psalm 135:14

I had to sit during the time set aside for my book signing without a single copy to give away. During that embarrassing time these verses were especially meaningful. I can only remember one other time in my life when I felt as humiliated as I did that afternoon. I used the time to talk to people about prayer and how to be more effective in doing it. My publisher and his staff stood by and watched. Later, when I asked my publisher to make several things right that I had been promised, He noted my good attitude and agreed to everything I requested

...Because the good hand of his God was upon him. For Ezra had set his heart to study the law of the Lord, and to practice it, and to teach His statutes and ordinances in Israel. Ezra 7:9b-10

The Lord's hand is on us when we set our hearts to learn God's

Word, to live it and to teach it to others. As I look back over the last year I see that when God has called on me to speak, He has blessed me, and others, with His presence and power.

He guides me in the paths of righteousness for His name's sake. Psalm 23:3b

By the world's measurements, the trip would have been considered a failure, but seen through spiritual eyes, I believe the mission was fulfilled. We all need God's direction in our daily lives. We need to know what to do in our own specific circumstances. It is in these times that the Word of God and our abiding relationship with the Father will guide us.

Verses given in connection to speaking engagements

I never deliver messages anymore out of my own self-designed thoughts. First, I wait for confirmation from the Lord to take a speaking engagement and then I wait for the message. Sometimes the Lord gives me a message before I know where and when it will be spoken. Sometimes the message comes later. One time, for the women of our church, the Lord gave the entire weekend of messages in one quiet time several months ahead of time. I always love it when He does that! But other times I have had to wait right up until the day of an event to know for sure what the Lord wants said. I have seen the difference, however, in what I can come up with on my own and what He delivers, and it's always worth waiting for His message.

As I finished preparing the messages for several speaking engagements in the fall of 2003, the Lord gave the following verses. They brought great comfort, as I didn't get a chance to finish the messages until the Friday of that very weekend. It was an incredible week of ministry! Without receiving this verse earlier in the week, I might have been troubled by how little study time I had been able to carve out.

Do not be anxious beforehand about what you are to say, but say whatever is given you in that hour; for it is not you who speak, but it is the Holy Spirit. Mark 13:11 Whoever speaks, let him speak, as it were, the utterances of God. I Peter 4:11a

Sometimes the enemy likes to try and intimidate me right before speaking. He makes me feel inadequate to break open the Word. I already know that any profound thoughts are not my own, but a gift from the One with unlimited understanding. Here are two good verses that have encouraged my heart:

Light is sown like seed for the righteous. Psalm 97:11a ...Even He who teaches man knowledge. Psalm 94:10b
(This is just a little phrase of a verse, but the thought snags my thinking every time. God teaches me all the knowledge that I get.)

I had been fasting prior to a particular speaking engagement. As I read the following verse, which is given twice in the passage for emphasis, it was as if the Lord was telling me that my physical weakness was going to be no obstacle for Him, and that He was going to add punch to the messages as a result of my obedience. He did just that! We had a marvelous altar call, where many responded to the Holy Spirit's work in their lives.

And your Father who sees in secret will repay you. Matthew 6:6b, 18b

This is one of the main themes of my speaking… to tell people about the great things the Lord has done for me. It's nice to know that's what the Lord wants me talking about, too.

Speak of all His wonders. Psalm 105:2b

Do you need direction in making a decision? Should you move? Should you sign that contract? Is God calling you to leave your job? Ask Him for His guidance and then, by all means, read the road signs in His Word. He will answer you. Your job is to keep your eyes and ears open for His signals.

Cautions concerning using the Word of God as a guide:

1. Other methods of hearing God's voice should work together to confirm what you believe God's Word to say. Many times someone has gotten off track by assuming that God was telling him to do thus and such, when it was from out in left field, as they completely ignored other checks and balances that He had provided.

2. Be careful not to take direction out of the context of God's complete Word. God may highlight a small phrase in a verse, but its meaning won't contradict the general message of the whole passage, much less His entire Word.

3. Because we are human, we have a tendency to look for what we want to see. It is so important to allow God's Word to speak freshly into our circumstances. Continually ask God to confirm His directions if you aren't sure. You have God's Word from James chapter one that He will always give us wisdom when we ask for it.

4. Time has a way of putting perspective to the things we believe God is saying. God doesn't change His mind and never makes a mistake. We, however, can misunderstand at times and misinterpret what the Lord is saying. In time, a fuller understanding can be given to us. So, when in doubt as to what to do, wait on the Lord.

For example: my friend Ruth was confused after her husband, Jon, died of cancer. During his treatment period, the verses she had felt the Holy Spirit highlight seemed to indicate a "rescuing." When Jon suddenly died there were many questions. Had she indeed been hearing God speak? How could what she felt the Bible was saying and reality have been so opposite? Dealing with these kinds of questions was not easy, but I knew God loved Ruth's honest, seeking heart. After almost two years of struggle the Lord gave her peace over the situation. After Jon's death, his business suffered a tremendous loss. Ruth can now see, by looking back on it all that perhaps the Lord was rescuing Jon from something that might have been too much for him to handle. The Lord gave her additional verses in the fall of 2003 that confirmed that He had indeed "rescued" Jon through death, rather than through healing. We heard a pastor say recently, "God is too good to be cruel and too wise to make mistakes." I believe this was the case in their lives.

My friend Michelle was making important decisions about her

time commitments in the fall of 2003. She wasn't sure if she should continue her own Bible study (which met in her home) and also be a part of the leadership for our church's Bible study for women. Her children were beginning at our school, which she knew would already demand more of her time (more homework help and volunteer opportunities would be requested). After this lesson on hearing God speak through His Word, she shared that He had already given her a verse, but she didn't know what He was trying to tell her to do through it. The verse was: *1 Corinthians 10:31: "So whether you eat or drink or whatever you do, do it all for the glory of God."* As she shared the verse with our discipleship group, the phrase "to the glory of God" stood out to us. We asked her, "What choice would give God the most glory?" She thought He would receive more glory if, in the demanding schedule, He was able to supply what was needed. The next morning in her quiet time the Lord gave her several verses that she felt confirmed that she should accept this new responsibility, like Colossians 3:16 *"Let the Word of Christ dwell in you richly as you teach..."* After watching Michelle serve in this ministry for the last year we know it was God's will for her to do it. He has received great glory from using her to help many women go deeper in their study of the Bible.

Right now while reading this chapter, you may feel, "How does this apply to me?" Verses that have spoken to my circumstances may not have any meaning for you. You may want to discount this whole notion of using God's Word to direct your daily decisions, but let me add another word of testimony on this subject. This lesson was written several months ago. As I write this closing paragraph today, six months later, I realize how powerful this lesson has been in my growth and progress over the last several months. I often apply specific verses to events or decisions for each day. I have been guided into good decisions many times, not by physical evidence, but by the theme that I read in my regular Bible study time. God wants to lead you. He opens His will like a puzzle. Some days you are given a few pieces, sometimes a whole section. At the proper time, the picture comes into focus and you know what action to take. Even it if means doing nothing at all. Smile.

Chapter 3 - Establish a Secret Place

But He Himself would often slip away to the wilderness and pray.
Luke 5:16

Where do you slip away to pray? I sometimes like to walk around a piece of property near our main church campus that we use for our youth ministry. It has a lot of open land that is semiprivate and I find great freedom in being able to pray out loud. Recently I shared my "secret place" with a friend that I was discipling. I had felt that morning that the Lord wanted her to see my special place to meet God. We walked around it and unloaded the cares of our hearts together before the Lord. It was a special moment for both of us.

Understanding our need for a place to meet God is essential in going deeper with God. The pressures and intensity of ministry will cause us to cry out for time with the One who sorts it all out. We need a place to run to - a lonely, deserted place where we can be alone with our Father. You can find one no matter where you are. Jesus said we can even find one in our closet. Smile.

I think it interesting that one of the places Jesus liked to pray was the place where He had faced an incredible spiritual battle. In the wilderness He had learned that God could sustain Him with more than mere bread. In the wilderness He had stood on the Word of God and had extinguished the fiery darts of the enemy. This is the place that called to Him when his neighbors wouldn't believe and his disciples all wanted to be in first place. When the multitude pressed in and the Pharisees laid traps, Jesus knew what to do. He ran to the "eye of the storm" and found peace. Sometimes he went to a wilderness and sometimes to a garden, but that doesn't matter. It was the One who waited for Him there who turned the storm into a place of peace.

When we first got married we had an abundance of furniture. My husband lived in a tiny two-bedroom duplex that was full of a myriad of furniture that friends had given him. I had my own apartment and it was filled with antiques my parents had given me. So, on one of the first days of our marriage, some rearranging took place. I could see the look of terror on my husband's face as he realized that all of his furniture was put out at the garage sale and all of my furniture was in the house. I couldn't understand why he was so attached to a bunch of old junk. Later I learned that an old stuffed chair, which looked uglier than sin, had been his "secret place." It was a chair that had weathered many spiritual battles of prayer. It was beautiful in his eyes because of what had been accomplished there. A church had been born on its cushions. Dreams for redeemed lives, a school, a retirement home, a home for unwed mothers and more had been seeded, through tears, on it. I'm happy we got to keep the dreams and that we've seen several of them fulfilled already. I'm still glad we got rid of the chair, though. Smile.

Do you slip away often to pray? Jesus said His yoke was easy and His burden was light. Do you realize that prayer is what makes it so? It is our highest need as human beings to be intimately connected to our Father and to find His perspective in the chaos of our lives. Jesus had found it more satisfying than food. And so, often, He would slip away to that place.

Today, find a place where you can begin seeding some dreams. Slip away and stand on some of God's promises for your life. Plant a garden of prayer in the middle of your wilderness and see what happens.

And in the early morning, while it was still dark, He arose and went out and departed to a lonely place, and was praying there. Mark 1:35

Then Jesus came with them to a place called Gethsemane, and said to His disciples, "Sit here while I go over there and pray." Matthew 26:36

And it came about that while He was praying in a certain place, after He had finished, one of His disciples said to Him, "Lord, teach us to pray just as John also taught his disciples." Luke 11:1

Chapter 4 - Pray Back Lives, Resources and Opportunities

Let your prayers pursue what is yours already

And they also took Lot, Abram's nephew, and his possessions and departed, for he was living in Sodom. Then a fugitive came and told Abram the Hebrew. Now he was living by the oaks of Mamre the Amorite, brother of Eshcol and brother of Aner, and these were allies with Abram. And when Abram heard that his relative had been taken captive, he led out his trained men, born in his house, three hundred and eighteen, and went in pursuit as far as Daniel And he divided his forces against them by night, he and his servants, and defeated them, and pursued them as far as Hobah, which is north of Damascus. And he brought back all the goods, and also brought back his relative Lot with his possessions, and also the women, and the people. Genesis 14:12-16

Abraham got some bad news one day. He was told that his nephew Lot, and the things that belonged to him, had been taken captive. His reply to these events is interesting. He didn't say, "Wow! That's too bad. What a bummer!" He didn't wring his hands and reply meekly, "Well, that must be God's will." He got together some folks who knew how to go to war and they brought back Lot and his possessions.

My friend, like Abraham, it's time for you to follow the trail of the enemy and return the spiritual lives of family members and the treasures of time and wisdom that the enemy has been pilfering from you. If you want to be "trained" in the skill of recovery, you will simply need to ask the Lord to "teach you to pray." His answer is always, "Yes."

One great way to learn to pray is to hang around people who do it. Smile. It doesn't matter who trained whom in this passage. Maybe some of Abe's men knew more about war than he did. That's OK. Perhaps he had trained them. It doesn't matter. What does matter is that when the time for war came, Abraham knew whom he could count on. He knew the men who didn't tremble under frightening situations. He knew the men who could be relied on to shoot a weapon accurately. He knew who was available for emergencies, and he used them.

Each morning of the week we begin our day, after our own personal time of prayer, in corporate prayer at the church. There is a group of four to ten people who show up to "cover" our church in prayer and to do spiritual warfare over what is "ours." Believe me when I say that our prayer groups are our church's greatest resource. Spiritual warfare is a fact of life. It has been and will be. But when you have warriors who are on the front line, equipped and ready to fight, you will be victorious.

These groups of people might look pretty ordinary to others: a housewife or two, a youth leader, a couple of staff people, etc. But in the spiritual realm they are known. Remember when the seven sons of Sceva were trying to remove demons from someone? *Acts 19:15 And the evil spirit answered and said to them, "I recognize Jesus, and I know about Paul, but who are you?"* The valiant warriors whom I get to pray with are big shots in the spiritual world. The enemy knows them. He has had to deal with their audacious prayers. His plans have been routed by their consistency. His purposes have been thwarted by their integrity, and his temptations have been routed by their knowledge of the Word. They are trained men and women. How did they get that way? They have given time to prayer and the Lord has answered their heart's desires with knowledge and experience.

So when I see trouble up ahead, I am not going to head into it alone. I head for the platoon of spiritually readied people who like pick-pocketing the enemy. We mount up our hopes on the promises of God's Word and head off to bring back lives, resources and opportunities that either are ours, or could be ours.

Prayer journal entry:

11/15/03 Began praying for Wendy's father to accept Christ. Up to now he has been adamantly opposed to even hearing about Jesus.

6/04 Ran into Wendy and she told the story of how her dad accepted Christ shortly before he died of cancer. Praise the Lord!

And when David and his men came to the city, behold, it was burned with fire, and their wives and their sons and their daughters had been taken captive. Then David and the people who were with him lifted their voices and wept until there was no strength in them to weep. Now David's two wives had been taken captive, Ahinoam the Jezreelitess and Abigail the widow of Nabal the Carmelite. Moreover David was greatly distressed because the people spoke of stoning him, for all the people were embittered, each one because of his sons and his daughters. But David strengthened himself in the Lord his God. Then David said to Abiathar the priest, the son of Ahimelech, "Please bring me the ephod." So Abiathar brought the ephod to David. And David inquired of the Lord, saying, "Shall I pursue this band? Shall I overtake them?" And He said to him, "Pursue, for you shall surely overtake them, and you shall surely rescue all." 1 Samuel 30:3-8

David is another man who comes home to find the enemy has ripped him off. His two wives had been taken: Abinoam and Abigail. Now I guess that David did have other wives, so he could have said, "That stinks!" and gone on with his day, but he knew that an excellent wife was a gift from the Lord. I'm sure he reflected on the circumstances that had brought Abigail, a woman of great wisdom, into his household. We don't know much about Abinoam, but she certainly had some special gifts also. Perhaps the thought passed through David's mind, "Why should the enemy have any of my wives?"

It's time to ask the same thing of ourselves. Why should the enemy have any of the lives of our children or our relatives? Why should he get any of the resources God has marked for us? Why should any opportunity that God wants us to have be thwarted? When we ask the Lord if we should go after wives, sons and daughters, His answer is the same to us that it was to David: *"Pursue, for you shall surely overtake them, and you shall surely rescue all."*

And David slaughtered them from the twilight until the evening of the next day; and not a man of them escaped, except four hundred young men who rode on camels and fled. So David recovered all that the Amalekites had taken, and rescued his two wives. But nothing of theirs was missing, whether small or great, sons or daughters, spoil or anything that they had taken for themselves; David brought it all back. 1 Samuel 30:17-19

I love the use of the word "all" in this passage. It denotes completeness. There is nothing of yours that the enemy is entitled to keep. What has he been holding onto that rightfully belongs to you? Mount up a force through prayer today and go and get it back.

A couple in our church had been praying for their runaway daughter for about a year when the request was shared with us. We began praying corporately to "entreat" the Lord to move on the situation. Year after year went by, but we continued to intercede. Four years later we came together on a Sunday morning for prayer, and there had been an answer to our prayers. The daughter had come back to her father's house to ask for help. You can imagine our joy, as prayer warriors, to know that the only contact that had been made with her over the past four years had been through the spiritual realm. She herself testified that if her mother and father had tried anytime before then to bring her home that she would have bolted and run.

And the anger of the Lord burned against Israel, and He gave them into the hands of plunderers who plundered them; and He sold them into the hands of their enemies around them, so that they could no longer stand before their enemies. Then the Lord raised up judges who delivered them from the hands of those who plundered them. Judges 2:14,16

Pray into being what could be yours for the glory of God and His kingdom

And when considerable time had passed and the voyage was now dangerous, since even the fast was already over, Paul began to admonish them, and said to them, "Men, I perceive that the voyage will certainly be attended with damage and great loss, not only of the cargo and the ship, but also of our lives." Acts 27:9-10

Paul teaches us to pray God's protection on our loved ones through his ordeal of a shipwreck at sea. First, he warned Julius and the ship's crew not to begin the journey at all. He had seen in the spiritual realm that there would be a future loss of life and property. But even though this had been revealed to him by God, he didn't stop there and take it for granted that this was God's determined will. Although lives would surely be lost without intervention, this did not mean it must happen. Sometimes God shows us the end result of a certain course of action, not so it will be reached, but so it can be avoided.

Paul began to intercede for the lives of his fellow prisoners, as well as the ship's crew. The reason I believe this is because, later, when an angel appeared to him, he told Paul that the lives of those traveling with him had been granted to him. This is where intercession makes the difference. It changes what could happen, into what should happen.

...Saying, "Do not be afraid, Paul; you must stand before Caesar; and behold, God has granted you all those who are sailing with you. Therefore, keep up your courage, men, for I believe God that it will turn out exactly as I have been told." Acts 27:24-25

I have had times when I doubted that God would save all my loved ones. I knew that there were many promises for "me and my children," but I wondered if there really were Scriptures that "bound" the Lord to help me in this regard. I must say that rereading the account of the Philippian jailer was an encouragement. Paul tells him to "Believe on the Lord Jesus Christ" and he would be saved... "and his household." Now remember, the jailer's family hadn't even heard the gospel message yet. It didn't take long for them to hear it and receive it, but what if they hadn't all accepted Christ that day; would that have negated the message Paul had given him? "And your household" was the spoken Word of God through Paul's lips. God can't be wrong! So even if the jailer's family hadn't accepted Christ that day, he could have stood on the promise. Some of us need to stand on that promise also. We've seen the enemy carry off our children, the peace in our households and missed opportunities. We can either stand weeping over the loss, or we can rouse a prayer posse and go after them.

I recently attended a funeral where a pastor friend shared about a woman who told her minister on her deathbed: "I have been praying for my four children to come to the Lord, but now that I'm dying, I guess the Lord isn't going to do it." The minister replied, "So what does your dying have to do with God's answering?" It was a good point: Whether or not you see God answer your prayer for the lives of loved ones is not connected to His answer. The minister went on to tell that after the woman's death all four children did come to the Lord. So, don't get discouraged by what you see. Just rest on what you've heard God say and be patient.

My husband is always teaching us Greek in his messages, and we have gotten familiar with the "subjunctive mood" which means "maybe it will and maybe it won't." Much of what we receive in this lifetime depends on our prayer life and the degree of trust we have in the living, active Word of God. I'm sure the enemy will try to carry off a little booty from your camp from time to time. The question is will you or won't you go after him and get it back?

Then He touched their eyes, saying, "It shall be done to you according to your faith." Matthew 9:29

Your job is to do the asking. So get out of that pity party! Mount up some trained men and women and go after what the enemy has laid claim to but is rightfully yours. Ruin his plans and reroute the resources that God wants you to have, and then use them according to God's plan and purposes. We must never allow these prayers to be self-centered but God-centered. Remember, self must face the cross daily or we will again fall prey to the enemy's schemes. Vigilance is absolutely critical as a warrior in the Army of God!

You do not have because you do not ask. James 4:2b

And all things you ask in prayer, believing, you shall receive. Matthew 21:22

Therefore I say to you, all things for which you pray and ask, believe that you have received them, and they shall be granted you. Mark 11:24

And He was saying, "Abba! Father! All things are possible for Thee" Mark 14:36a

The Father loves the Son, and has given all things into His hand. John 3:35

He who did not spare His own Son, but delivered Him up for us all, how will He not also with Him freely give us all things? Romans 8:32

So then let no one boast in men. For all things belong to you, whether Paul or Apollos or Cephas or the world or life or death or things present or things to come; all things belong to you, and you belong to Christ; and Christ belongs to God. I Corinthians 3:21-23

These verses and others show us that nothing is out of reach for our prayers!

Pray that God's people will get back what the enemy has been using

Now the sons of Israel had done according to the word of Moses, for they had requested from the Egyptians articles of silver and articles of gold, and clothing; and the Lord had given the people favor in the sight of the Egyptians, so that they let them have their request. Thus they plundered the Egyptians. Exodus 12:35-36

When you are at war, one of the main targets is the supply line of the enemy. I remember reading about the Civil War and the strategy used to cut off the enemy's supplies in order to end the war sooner. In our spiritual conflict, this is one of the places where we want to aim our prayers. Proverbs 13:22b promises: *"And the wealth of the sinner is stored up for the righteous. "* I don't know about you, but when I think that the enemy is using up something that God has ear-marked for me, I get angry. The more resources the enemy has, the more damage he can do to the Lord's work. Think about the vast fortunes that have been amassed through the sale of pornography, drugs, gambling and other sleazy industries. Those profits "feed" more of the enemy's work. But God has told me that, *"The sinner's wealth is stored up for the righteous. "* So I have a choice to make in my prayers. I can resign myself to all of the opportunities and resources the enemy has, or I can begin to rest in the promise of God's Word, and pursue what God wants to do for me, His child.

For to a person who is good in His sight He has given wisdom and knowledge and joy, while to the sinner He has given the task of gathering and collecting so that he may give to one who is good in God's sight. This too is vanity and striving after wind. Ecclesiastes 2:26

Then it shall come about when the Lord your God brings you into the land which He swore to your fathers, Abraham, Isaac and Jacob, to give you, great and splendid cities which you did not build, and houses full of all good things which you did not fill, and hewn cisterns which you did not dig, vineyards and olive trees which you did not plant, and you shall eat and be satisfied, then watch yourself, lest you forget the Lord who brought you from the land of Egypt, out of the house of slavery. Deuteronomy 6:10-12

The children of Israel had been learning about God's supply for forty years, but finally the day came when they entered the Promised Land. They didn't at that point have the time to plant vineyards, to build houses and to fill their own needs. But because the Lord in-tended for them to have the land and its produce, and as they put their foot down, treading on new areas of resource and property, the Lord allowed them to annihilate the enemy and to move into houses that were already built, with barns that were already full of food and sup-plies. One day these resources were supporting sodomy, idolatry and rebellion. The next day they were feeding God's people and His work.

The crucial part is that God relied on the children of Israel to decide how much territory they could retrieve. Look around at what the enemy is accomplishing with his resources. Does it make you a little angry? Today allow your prayers to blow up his line of supply. Start treading, through your intercession, on what rightfully belongs to the Kingdom of God and pray for the return of what has been taken from you.

One of my favorite passages is found in I Kings chapter 7.

When these lepers came to the outskirts of the camp, they entered one tent and ate and drank, and carried from there silver and gold and clothes, and went and hid them; and they returned and entered another tent and carried from there also, and went and hid them. Then they said to one another, "We are not doing right. This day is a day of good news, but we are keeping silent; if we wait until morning light, punishment will overtake us. Now therefore come, let us go and tell the king's household." So they came and called to the gatekeepers of the city, and they told them, saying, "We came to the camp of the Arameans, and behold, there was no one there, nor the voice of man, only the horses tied and the donkeys tied, and the tents just as they were." And the gatekeepers called, and told it within the king's household. 2 Kings 7:8-11

Just before this passage takes place, we see a dismal situation. Israel was surrounded by the enemy. They were in such a desperate famine that people were eating dove's dung. You would have to be really hungry for that! Just outside the city walls, the enemy had plenty to eat. He had silver, gold, horses and tents. God caused the army of the Arameans to hear a sound that made them all run away and, as the four lepers determined that their only hope was to turn themselves in and to hope for mercy from their enemy, they stumbled upon empty tents full of good things. At first they were self-focused, but soon they realized that selfishness was unacceptable. So they informed the king of the bounty available. In time somebody believed their report that there were horses, donkeys, food and clothing over in the enemy's camp. The day came when someone went over to see if what the lepers were saying was true and they found a bountiful amount of booty was available for the taking, and as a result the nation of Israel didn't starve to death.

It is important to note here that the Lord does not unleash the resources of the enemy for selfish purposes. He tells us that in James 4:3, *"You ask and do not receive, because you ask with wrong motives, so that you may spend it on your pleasures."* The Lord is able to sniff out self-focused prayers in no time and they are unanswered. But if you see the work of God living in a famine state and the enemy is feasting, it's time to stalk up to his camp, enter his tents of resource, and bring back some booty. The Lord will help you in this because He's not happy anytime the enemy gains the advantage over His people.

"You will tread down the wicked, for they will be ashes under the soles of your feet on the day which I am preparing," says the Lord of hosts. Malachi 4:3

Every place on which the sole of your foot treads, I have given it to you, just as I spoke to Moses. Joshua 1:3

Chapter 5 - Seek the God of the Impossible in Marriage

After these things Jesus manifested Himself again to the disciples at the Sea of Tiberias, and He manifested Himself in this way. There were together Simon Peter, and Thomas called Didymus, and Nathanael of Cana in Galilee, and the sons of Zebedee, and two others of His disciples. Simon Peter said to them, "I am going fishing." They said to him, "We will also come with you." They went out, and got into the boat; and that night they caught nothing. But when the day was now breaking, Jesus stood on the beach; yet the disciples did not know that it was Jesus. Jesus therefore said to them, "Children, you do not have any fish, do you?" They answered Him, "No." And He said to them, "Cast the net on the right-hand side of the boat, and you will find a catch." They cast therefore, and then they were not able to haul it in because of the great number of fish. That disciple therefore whom Jesus loved said to Peter, "It is the Lord." And so when Simon Peter heard that it was the Lord, he put his outer garment on (for he was stripped for work), and threw himself into the sea. But the other disciples came in the little boat, for they were not far from the land, but about one hundred yards away, dragging the net full of fish. And so when they got out upon the land, they saw a charcoal fire already laid, and fish placed on it, and bread. Jesus said to them, "Bring some of the fish which you have now caught." Simon Peter went up, and drew the net to land, full of large fish, a hundred and fifty-three; and although there were so many, the net was not torn. Jesus said to them, "Come and have breakfast." None of the disciples ventured to question Him, "Who are You?" knowing that it was the Lord. Jesus came and took the bread, and gave them, and the fish likewise. This is now the third time that Jesus was manifested to the disciples, after He was raised from the dead. John 21:1-14

Three questions come to mind about this passage:
1. Where did Jesus get His fish?
2. How did the disciples get their fish?
3. Why did Jesus require the disciples to give Him some of their fish?

Where did Jesus get His fish? He had no fishing pole and no boat. Yet the fire had freshly caught fish on it when the disciples came to shore. Jesus had not spent all night fishing, yet here was the product of fishing, minus the labor.

I suspect it has something in common with the time that Peter needed tax money? *However, so that we do not offend them, go to the sea and throw in a hook, and take the first fish that comes up; and when you open its mouth, you will find a shekel. Take that and give it to them for you and Me. Matthew 17:27* Jesus told Peter to pull up the first fish and look in its mouth. He found a coin and paid their taxes. Think about it: Jesus commanded a fish to swallow a coin, to be on a certain beach at a certain time and to be caught by Peter's hook. The fish obeyed!

Jesus commands fish and they obey. He can command breakfast to show up without effort. He is God Almighty. He can do what no man could ever dream of accomplishing. He takes the impossible and makes it mundane.

"Ah Lord God! Behold, Thou hast made the heavens and the earth by Thy great power and by Thine outstretched arm! Nothing is too difficult for Thee." Jeremiah 32:17 "Behold, I am the Lord, the God of all flesh; is anything too difficult for Me?" Jeremiah 32:27

God can help with impossible marriage situations

This is an important concept in relation to marriage. When we are in connection with Almighty God, we can never overestimate His abilities. We can only underestimate them. He can do the impossible in an instant. Tax problems are solved in a sentence. Questions like, "What will we eat today?" are solved with fresh fish on the grill or in baskets with bread.

There is no problem you can ever face in your marriage that the God of the Impossible cannot solve. All around us are human billboards attesting to God's power. Drugs, adultery, abuse and anger can all be obliterated from a life when Jesus walks in. For some it is miraculous, in an instant. For others, the transformation is one step

40

at a time like when the Israelites conquered the Promised Land. The Lord could obliterate all of our marriage problems with a miracle, but He usually doesn't. Why? To find the answer let's keep asking questions.

Where did the disciples get their fish? The fish were there in the lake all the time, but the disciples hadn't been able to catch them yet. Their human methods were inadequate for catching these crafty fish. They kept eluding the nets. Although the disciples were putting forth a great deal of effort, they kept coming up with empty nets.

Can you understand the frustrations and emotions of fishermen who have caught no fish? Perhaps you feel some of this frustration in your marriage relationship right now. You, like the disciples, are fully devoted followers. You are giving it all you have but you don't seem to have caught anything yet. Peace is escaping your home. Blessing and relational bliss are eluding you.

In this situation what is needed is direction from the Lord: "Try the other side of the boat." Were there really more fish on one side of the boat than on the other? Probably not the minute before Jesus gave the command. But the moment Jesus commanded the disciples to go to the other side of the boat, there was a command understood by fish to move there also. Fish have to obey Jesus.

Now why did Jesus do this? First of all, He already knew what the disciples needed even before they did. He knew that for the next forty days they would need to focus their attention on a risen Lord, and not on feeding their families. He knew that until Pentecost when the amount of Christians and offerings would dramatically increase, these disciples and their families would need to eat. (After the church was established there would be support for these men and their families. We don't know about any other provision during this interim period, other than the mighty catch of fish.) They would be seeking first the Kingdom of God through corporate prayer and Bible study, and He had already laid the resources for them to do this, and still pay the bills.

So Jesus stepped into His own created order and spoke change. He commanded these fish to be caught. The only reason the fish were on the other side was because Jesus had the authority to command them to be there and the disciples needed to learn a lesson about faith.

Following Jesus' direction produced what these families needed. Now this is a place we need to stop for a while, because following Jesus' commands are not always easy. First, we have the problem with our "understanding." We are so limited in our brain capacity we can't even figure out why Jesus tells us to do certain things.

I was asked one night to speak to the women of our church on marriage. I expected the Lord to use some word pictures that women would relate to and some lessons I knew He had taught me over the years. While I was waiting for His direction, one morning the Lord gave this lesson from John 21. As the days neared when I was going to have to teach, I again implored the Lord to show me what He wanted said to the women. Imagine my surprise when He said that He wanted me to share these thoughts on fishing. My mind couldn't see why, but as I began to think about marriage the three points began to make sense. There are times in counseling when with our human eyes a marriage looks shipwrecked. It's all we can do to plaster a veneer of faith across the circumstances. It's then we need to remember the God who commands fish and men. He is the One who produces breakfast from nothing and the One who knows how to speak miracles into reality.

Prayer journal entry:

One Friday Ike and I met with a couple whose marriage seemed to be over. Soon after we saw the Lord do a miraculous work that got them back on track. (Prayer was at the root of the change.)

But the second point of this message is important also. The Savior could not only do the impossible Himself; He could also direct ordinary, human beings to do the same. With His direction, failing men became successful fishermen. If there is anything we need to hold on to in dealing with the tough issues of marriage, it is this: Jesus can tell us what we need to do to fix them.

One thing Ike and I have learned in marriage counseling over the years is this: when two believers come into the presence of the Holy Spirit with a genuine desire to obey His direction, there are usually answers, plans and progress. However, many times one person is stuck in self and disobedience. Our prayers and counsel from the Word of God are the pry bars that can unjam their thinking, if they are willing. But sometimes adults, like children, sit in the corner and suck their thumbs. The process may take years of prayer, talking, loving and trying. If this is where you are right now, take hope. God can command men and women as well as fish. We see from the lives of the prodigal son and Jonah that God is committed to being obeyed and He is willing to wait out the process for a son or daughter to "come home" in their thinking.

Many of the marriage problems we see in counseling are caused by a couple being unequally yoked. I was talking with a teller at my bank the other day. On a previous visit she had told me that she was a Christian and was praying for "her prince." When I asked her how that prayer request was coming along, she began to share about a man in her life. I asked, "Is he a Christian?" She answered, "Well no, but…" "Then he's not your prince," I said matter-of-factly. Too many Christians ignore the Word of God and end up facing years of heartache by trying to convince themselves that they can live the rest of their lives in intimacy with someone who doesn't love their Savior. I told the teller that unless she wants to spend the rest of her life turning on the light and having her husband turn it off, she'd better look elsewhere for her prince. Unfortunately, many times the consequences of ignoring God's command to not become yoked with someone who isn't His child involves a terrible payment plan. If this is where you are, let me save you hours of time on your knees. This is not God's will for your life.

Disclaimer: there are many variables that affect marriages, and this book is not meant to address them. It is primarily meant to focus our attention on the One who can affect any marriage and bring about good from any experience.

I was thinking about the application for the third part of this story, that Jesus required the disciples to give Him some of their fish. Why does the Lord let limited human fishermen catch fish? I think it is so they will acknowledge Him and His lordship. When we put some of our fish on the sacrificial barbecue, it helps us remember the significant God-things that He has done in our lives. When we have times in our marriage where we can relate to "fishing all night and coming up empty" and then remember the mornings where we ate our fill of fresh fish, we should willingly respond with the offering of our time, resources and honor to the One who made those feasts possible. This is Jesus' favorite breakfast. He loves to see couples who have gone through difficulties willing to share their "breakfast" with others. He smiles when we share the tough nights where we tried and tried and came up empty, so that we can give Him glory because we have enjoyed plenty at His grill.

Blessed be the God and Father of our Lord Jesus Christ, the Father of mercies and God of all comfort, who comforts us in all our affliction so that we will be able to comfort those who are in any affliction with the comfort with which we ourselves are comforted by God. 2 Corinthians 1:3-4

The relationship of a couple at our church was in shambles. He had left her, and the family was reeling from the effects. Shortly, this family was in disarray. Still, the wife held on. She continued to pray and hope. The Lord got a hold of the husband's life and radically brought about transformation and confession. They renewed their marriage vows in front of a couple hundred witnesses at a recent Valentine's Banquet and there was not a dry eye in the house. Now, as I see them serving as the team God intended, I am glad I serve the God of the Impossible. (If you are in a difficult place in your marriage right now, keep focusing on the fish on the barbecue!)

So why did Jesus require the disciples to give Him some of their fish? Remember, He already had some fish frying. Why did He need more? Had He failed to know how many people would be coming for breakfast? Was He caught shorthanded on supplies? No. He simply wanted them to eat some of the fish that they knew He had commanded them to catch.

Jesus knows that there is a special victory that comes with accomplishment. Although the disciples had simply obeyed Jesus' command, He wanted them to relish the moment. He wanted them to revel in the miracle that occurred when they simply followed orders. He wanted them to know that even when they couldn't understand the reasoning behind the voice, they could always trust its guidance. I think He also wanted an offering, a tithe of what He had provided. He wanted the honor of eating some of the fish He had provided for them.

Let us remember in dealing with all of life's challenges that Jesus knows where the fish are. Jesus knows how to help us catch fish. Jesus knows that we need to acknowledge who brings the fish. So He lets us lay some of our catch on the grill and eat it. The meal of life's wisdom is not dropped into our laps. We catch truth one fish at a time. We learn how to deal with each other one experience at a time. Yes, we get to hold up the fish for the camera, but we know who really pulled the whole event off. It is the Lord, the one who feeds us with food that sustains.

Not long ago my daughter was having a birthday party at a ceramic shop. They were painting animals and the owner gently asked the girls, "Do you want me to help you with those eyes?" Some of them hesitated. Many of my daughter's friends come from families with significant arts and crafts skills. At last they said, "Yes," and she began to go to work. I thought, "How ludicrous!" Here she is with all her abilities and skills, offering to help, and here they are with all their need and helplessness hesitating for even a minute to accept it. But so it is with God. He knows where the fish are. He has the authority to make them all move to the left side of the boat, and He asks, "Do you want some help with that marriage?" We sometimes hesitate, thinking that the problems are within our own abilities to sort out and fix.

And He said to them, "Cast the net on the right-hand side of the boat, and you will find a catch." They cast therefore, and then they were not able to haul it in because of the great number of fish. John 21:6

Never before had they ever experienced such a catch. But they would have missed it if they had failed to follow Jesus' instructions. Jesus knows what I need to do to be effective in my witnessing, in my marriage and in my job. I can hold on to my nets, my usual methods and position, or I can listen for the voice of the One who knows how to bring up a miracle catch by my simply following orders.

Now there is another problem here. Over the years we have counseled some hardheads that could quote scripture like it was their telephone number, but who had rotten marriages. There were times, when facing these characters in the presence of the Holy Spirit, that I doubted whether they had ever had a true conversion to Jesus. You see, we can't belong to God without one earmarking characteristic: compassion. We can claim relationship, like the Pharisees, but if we'd rather see a sick woman stay sick, because it would mess up our neat Sabbath rules, then we don't really know Jesus. That's why the quality of compassion is the root of all the good stuff Jesus wants to teach His disciples. That's why the story of the Good Samaritan was important. And that's why whenever we see Jesus encounter a hurting individual He lets us peek into His heart to see that what moves Him to action: His compassion for others.

And the synagogue official, indignant because Jesus had healed on the Sabbath, began saying to the multitude in response, "There are six days in which work should be done; therefore come during them and get healed, and not on the Sabbath day." But the Lord answered him and said, "You hypocrites, does not each of you on the Sabbath untie his ox or his donkey from the stall, and lead him away to water him?" And this woman, a daughter of Abraham as she is, whom

Satan has bound for eighteen long years, should she not have been released from this bond on the Sabbath day?" Luke 13:14-16

Compassion is the family characteristic of our Lord that spans the generations. That's why John tells us that we can't know God and hate our brother. That's why Jesus weeps over His people and His city. Even though He's been wronged by lies, wronged by physical pain and wronged, ultimately, by disgrace, He could turn and say "Father, forgive them." Wow! There is a lot of power in those words.

If compassion is in short supply in your heart right now, you are an empty supply closet for the work God wants to accomplish in your marriage. Stop right now and ask for a new supply from the One who never runs out.

If you're thinking about getting married, look for this quality in your future spouse. Is he or she tenderhearted in God's presence? Does the Holy Spirit have the control of his or her heart now? If so, perhaps this is the person God is leading you to marry. There will be many more things to look for, but this one is one of the highest requirements I believe every Christian should look for: sensitivity to the Holy Spirit's work and a responsive, compassionate and obedient heart.

You'll find the Almighty can do so much in and through your marriage as you meditate on the three aspects of this Scripture passage: There are things only God can do for your marriage, i.e. the miraculous fish that Jesus had cooking. There are things God can help you do for your marriage, i.e. the fish Jesus directed the disciples to catch. And finally, there are things God has allowed you to experience so you can help others in their marriages, i.e. that are represented by the fish we lay on Jesus' grill. Sometimes it's the sacrifice of praise and glory given in a testimony. Sometimes the meal is made up of all the things you tried in your own power to make your marriage work that failed. Sometimes the feast is provided by the "yeses" you gave God that delighted in the product and progress for your relationship. One way or the other, you will enjoy the meal.

For how do you know, O wife, whether you will save your husband? Or how do you know, O husband, whether you will save your wife? 1 Corinthians 7:16

Chapter 6 - Seek the God of the Impossible in Illness

Since the beginning of time it has never been heard that anyone opened the eyes of a person born blind. John 9:32

And on the basis of faith in His name, it is the name of Jesus which has strengthened this man whom you see and know; and the faith which comes through Him has given him this perfect health in the presence of you all. Acts 3:16

One of the most challenging areas to learn to pray in is that of sickness. Anyone who has walked with God for any period of time can tell you that sometimes God heals sickness and sometimes He does not. Paul was used to heal many, but his own "thorn in the flesh" was not healed. He had to leave his good friend Epaphroditus in a seriously ill condition without a healing. This leaves Christians with a dilemma. How do we pray when someone is ill? I have some brothers and sisters that believe every sickness can be commanded to "leave," but I don't agree. Many times illness and even death can bring more glory to God than healing. But I also believe that we don't see as many healings as we could because of a lack of faith.

Some Christians don't even ask for a physical healing in their illness. They resign themselves to living with whatever trial they are facing. They assume that all sickness is allowed by God and should be accepted. I disagree. We see in the encounter of Job that the source of the illness he suffered came from the enemy and that God's ultimate purpose was for its removal. But we get into trouble if we think that we are smarter than God, and that He can't use sickness or even death to accomplish His purposes.

I find in 1 John that my job is simply to ask

Until now you have asked for nothing in My name; ask and you will receive, so that your joy may be made full. John 16:24 You do not have because you do not ask. James 4:2b

God's method of "asking" is found in *James 5:14 Is anyone among you sick? Then he must call for the elders of the church and they are to pray over him, anointing him with oil in the name of the Lord.* Now if we as a church were living in obedience to these instructions, wouldn't our "programming" have to reflect it? If everyone who was sick was requesting to be anointed with oil and prayed over, wouldn't that take a huge amount of time each week? Unfortunately not many ever request this. Why? Is it pride? Is it inconvenience? Is it fear? I don't know the motivations. I do know that only a few, those with the most severe illnesses, ever ask for this kind of prayer.

We read in *1 Corinthians 11:30: For this reason many among you are weak and sick, and a number sleep.* Many were sick because they received communion without confessing their sins. This kind of sickness would require corporate humility as well as prayer to be removed. Who knows what kinds of sickness are in our churches today, not as a result of the enemy's testing, but as a result of sin and stubbornness?

The disciples obeyed Jesus' instructions and saw great results: *And they were casting out many demons and were anointing with oil many sick people and healing them. Mark 6:13*

It is my job to make sure my faith is active and ready

Faith is an essential element in the healings of the Bible, and it is the characteristic we most need to concern ourselves with and then, leave the results in the hands of the Master Healer. For instance, the lame man had to sit by the Gate Beautiful for thirty-eight years so that the Son of God could be honored as the highest Healer.[1] The blind man had been that way from birth so God could get glory in an instant.[2]

There is no prayer request in the Bible deader than the one Martha had for her brother Lazarus. He was in the grave, along with all her hope, when Jesus said to her: *"Did I not say to you if you believe, you will see the glory of God?" John 11:40*

It is difficult to pray with faith for someone's healing, see him or her die and still remain faithful for the next person who needs healing. Our church never had a member die in fifteen years (this is because we were a younger congregation) until 2004 when we had several deaths in just a couple of months. It was especially difficult to see our friend, Gary, battle leukemia for an entire year and finally pass away. Many of us really believed the Lord would heal him. His work with the Gideons was crucial to the Kingdom and to our human minds it made sense that God would heal him. However, God knew better. I will be asking God, "Why?" in Heaven some day.

We have to remove ourselves from the equation if we are to have fresh faith for the next person. We must focus on the God of the impossible as well as the God of all knowledge. We must present ourselves with faith each time there is a challenge, but remember that we are not in the driver's seat of the adventure.

It's the Father's job to decide what answer will suit His purposes best

Doctors told one gentleman in our church to go home and put his affairs in order. Surgery revealed cancer, and he didn't have much time. He, in obedience, asked the elders of our church to pray. He told his wife on the way to the car afterwards, "Honey, the Lord just healed me." A second battery of tests revealed no trace of cancer. Here was one of those amazing times God intervened.

On another occasion we were asked to pray for a little eight-year old girl who had recently been diagnosed with leukemia. Our church did so and later, we found that at the hospital there had been a mix-up of medical records. The little girl we had been praying for did not have leukemia at all. This prompted us to pray for the unknown child who did have the disease.

If each person who was ill came with a sticker on their forehead showing you how the Lord would deal with their case, you could know better how to pray, i.e. this one will be healed, this one will die, etc. But they don't. That is why we must continue to pray for them over the long haul and seek God's direction in how to pray for them.

When my friend Renee, who had fought cancer and won, found out eight years later that it was back and the doctors had given her only a couple of months to live, we ran to the Lord. I don't have the ability to read God's mind. Who am I to say He could only receive glory from her life and not her death. However, I am continuing to meditate on the promises of God's Word. We do not know the final outcome of her situation yet, but when the doctor's walk out, it's the time for Jesus to walk in. And these kind of impossible situations are just what He uses to show His mighty power, so we continue to ask for a complete healing.

God's Word has brought comfort and encouragement to our hearts in the case of my husband's illness. In my first book I shared about some eating problems that my husband, Ike, was dealing with. However, in 2003 he was diagnosed with fibromyalgia and chronic fatigue syndrome. Each day his health declines rapidly, and I want to pray effectively in the midst of the situation. Below are some of the verses the Lord used to comfort my heart. Although I still do not know how this situation will turn out, I can take courage through the truths these verses offer me. They also give me many clues in how to pray for him.

This illness is one that has turned out to give God much glory. Every Sunday and Wednesday we, as a congregation, get to watch a man weak with pain get up and become an instrument of the Holy Spirit's anointing. Ike preaches with power and conviction and then sits back down in weakness and helplessness. What a miracle we witness as we watch! I wonder if God could get more glory through one big miracle of healing as He does each week through these weekly mini-miracles.

In Thee our fathers trusted; they trusted, and Thou didst deliver them. To Thee they cried out, and were delivered; in Thee they trusted, and were not disappointed. Psalm 22:4-5

Commit yourself to the Lord; let Him deliver him; let Him rescue him, because He delights in him. Psalm 22:8

I will tell of Thy name to my brethren; in the midst of the assembly I will praise Thee. You who fear the Lord, praise Him; all you descendants of Jacob, glorify Him, and stand in awe of Him, all you descendants of Israel. For He has not despised nor abhorred the affliction of the afflicted; neither has He hidden His face from him; but when he cried to Him for help, He heard. From Thee comes my praise in the great assembly; I shall pay my vows before those who fear Him. The afflicted shall eat and be satisfied; those who seek Him will praise the Lord. Let your heart live forever! Psalm 22:22-26

Even though I walk in the valley of the shadow of death, I will fear no evil, for Thou art with me. Psalm 23:4

I will instruct you and teach you in the way which you should go; I will counsel you with My eye upon you. Psalm 32:8

In this you greatly rejoice, even though now for a little while, if necessary, you have been distressed by various trials, that the proof of your faith, being more precious than gold which is perishable, even though tested by fire, may be found to result in praise and glory and honor at the revelation of Jesus Christ. I Peter 1:6-7

He does not delight in the strength of the horse; He takes no pleasure in the legs of a man. The Lord takes pleasure in those who fear Him, in hose who hope in His mercy. Psalm 147:10-11 NKJ

Note: I thought this verse was great, because Ike's legs don't work like they used to. Even short distances of walking tire him out, but this verse says that God isn't impressed if he can walk or not. But it gives God great pleasure to see us trust Him. Smile.

For I consider that the sufferings of the present time are not worthy to be compared with the glory which shall be revealed in us. Romans 8:18 NKJ

Heal me, O Lord, and I shall be healed; save me, and I shall be saved. For You are my praise. Jeremiah 13:14

For we know that if our earthly house, this tent, is destroyed, we have a building from God, a house not made of hands, eternal in the Heavens.. 2 Corinthians 5:11

And Mary said, "Behold, the bond slave of the Lord. Be it done to me according to Thy word." Luke 1:38a

For not one of us lives for himself, and not one dies for himself; for if we live, we live for the Lord, or if we die, we die for the Lord; therefore whether we live or die, we are the Lord's. Romans 14:7-8

Sickness increases our prayer life

One reason God allows sickness is to increase our prayer lives. He knows that when we care, we pray. The Apostle Paul talks about a time in his ministry when he despaired even of life itself. We are not told what the situation is, whether emotional or physical. But we do know this: Paul was delivered from this trial through the prayers of many. He testifies in 2 Corinthians chapter one that the Christians of Corinth were helping him in the struggle. Here they were miles away, and yet their prayers were making a difference in his daily existence.

Indeed, we had the sentence of death within ourselves so that we would not trust in ourselves, but in God who raises the dead; who delivered us from so great a peril of death, and will deliver us, He on whom we have set our hope. And He will yet deliver us, you also joining in helping us through your prayers, so that thanks may be given by many persons on our behalf for the favor bestowed on us through the prayers of many. 2 Corinthians 1:9-11

All around us are people whose daily existence is a struggle. My friend Lucy is challenged by multiple sclerosis. Each day for her is spent in a wheel chair. Lucy has told me about the days of ministry that she and her husband Dave have enjoyed. In the past, her home was a place for Bible study and fellowship. She served her church in many ways. Now, every day I'm sure she can relate to Paul's wording in verse nine, "we had the sentence of death within ourselves." For me, it is good to know that my prayers can make a difference in Lucy's life. When the battle is overwhelming, the prayers of many can turn the tide.

Who is being "helped" today by your prayers? Whose personal battle is being won because you are there, like Aaron and Hur, to hold them up in prayer?

But Moses' hands were heavy. Then they took a stone and put it under him, and he sat on it; and Aaron and Hur supported his hands, one on one side and one on the other. Thus his hands were steady until the sun set. Exodus 17:12

One year as I attended our Southern Baptist pastor's wives retreat, we heard an outstanding testimony of healing from Denise Drake. Her husband Ken had gone from being perfectly healthy to being confined in a hospital bed in the middle of their living room. The illness began with pain in his feet. There came a time when Ken could not wear shoes, even to preach. His congregation was praying for him and understood the situation, but his condition continued to worsen. Ken experienced tremendous pain even from something as slight as a breeze blowing across him while lying in bed. Soon Ken could no longer continue in the challenges of ministry and Denise went back to work to support their family. Their two children took turns staying home from school to care for their father and many trips to specialists took place.

During this time there was a force of prayer going up for Ken all over the world. It is true that there was no physical evidence that this prayer was helping Ken. This is what the enemy wants us to believe: that whatever is going to happen is inevitable and that our prayers do not change the course of events. This is why we must persevere in our prayers. An all-night prayer meeting saw Peter delivered from prison and our all-out times of intercession can bring healing.

One day as Denise was hurrying home to change clothes before a worship rehearsal at her church, which was a change to her normal routine, she received a phone call from her pastor. He said that some pastors from South America, who had been involved with revival and prayer, were visiting and he wanted them to pray over Ken. He asked if that would be possible. Denise felt a twinge of excitement and faith as they prepared Ken to receive company. There in their little living room these pastors began to pray. As Denise tells the story, she couldn't help but peak during their prayers and what she saw amazed her. She saw Ken's legs begin to quiver. In a few minutes they were all gazing at a modern day miracle. Ken was completely healed! This took place years ago and Ken has been an active, healthy minister since the time of his healing. Denise and Ken have been used to teach many about the power of prayer and many around the world have had their faith stretched through the experience. Praise God who can do the impossible! Praise God who uses our prayers to change things! Isn't it wonderful that God allowed many people to participate in this fantastic work through their prayers?

Today aim your prayers at some impossible illnesses and believe. Grab a brother or sister in the Lord and pray over something the enemy says is "out of reach."

Chapter 7 - Seek the God of the Impossible and Reaching the Lost

If you have read my first book, <u>Waiting at the Window</u>, you know that I have been praying for a special friend to come to Christ for a long time. I have interceded for him for more than four years now. (His family has been praying even longer.) Take courage if you are praying for someone's salvation. We believe our friend is almost there.

One day, when we had passed the four-year anniversary mark or our prayers for him, I thought faithlessly, "Maybe he will never come to You, Lord." I wondered out loud if my prayers could actually affect the human will of another. It was in that quiet time that God responded with some truths from His Word.

For just as the Father raises the dead and gives them life, even so the Son also gives life to whom He wishes. John 5:21 "Truly, truly, I say to you, he who hears My word, and believes Him who sent Me, has eternal life, and does not come into judgment, but has passed out of death into life." John 5:24 And He was saying, "For this reason I have said to you, that no one can come to Me, unless it has been granted him from the Father." John 6:65 ...who were born not of blood, nor of the will of the flesh, nor of the will of man, but of God. John 1:13

First, the Lord opened up John 5:21 to my heart. He gave me the example of a corpse to show me how helpless an unsaved person really is. A dead man can't say, "Save me!" He can't say, "I'd like to be alive now." But God, who can bring dead men to life, can prick his heart and he can respond. Dr. Henry Blackaby has taught us through his book, <u>Experiencing God</u>, that daily the Father is at work all around us doing that very thing.

A pastor friend of mine, Rick Grooms, shared his testimony with me not long ago. Rick's wife, Debbie, was a believer and he sometimes attended church with her before his conversion. When the communion elements were passed, he knew enough about God's

Word not to take communion without being a believer. He wanted to believe in God, but he didn't have enough faith and he wasn't going to fake it. Well on one particular morning as communion was being passed, Rick began to have a new thought, "Jesus died for me." Suddenly, in an instant he realized, "I do believe." Shortly after he realized that for the first time in his life he could take communion because he believed the fact that Jesus died for him. God gave Rick what he had wanted: a little seed of faith to believe. God did not override Rick's own free will, but He empowered Rick's desire to believe.

My prayer: That's all my friend needs, God, a little seed of faith to believe. He's dead to spiritual things, but you can just give him the seed of faith he needs to bring him to the salvation.

I am not attempting to settle the great theological debates of all time with this simple book on prayer. I do want to show that we can make a difference in the outcome of the salvation of others through our prayers.

The story is told that George Mueller prayed for salvation for fifty men regularly and that over the years he had seen all but two of them accept Christ. Shortly before George died one of the last two became a Christian and after his death, the final man confessed his faith in Jesus Christ.

Who are you praying for today that needs Christ? Who will enter the gates of Heaven tomorrow as a result of your intercession today? Make a "hit" list. Write down the names of those that you want to find Christ and battle for their lives in your secret place today.

But thanks be to God, who always leads us in triumph in Christ, and manifests through us the sweet aroma of the knowledge of Him in every place. For we are a fragrance of Christ to God among those who are being saved and among those who are perishing; to the one

an aroma from death to death, to the other an aroma from life to life.
And who is adequate for these things? 2 Corinthians 2:14-16

Prayer journal entry:

Many of us began to pray for a Mormon lady whose children attended our school. On January 9, 2001, I noted on my prayer list that she was now considering becoming a Christian. In the year 2002 she gave her heart to the Lord and now she serves on our school staff. Praise the Lord!

Back in the year 2000, a friend of mine and I started praying for her husband to come to know God. He was adamant about not coming to church, so this prayer request looked impossible. My friend, Becky, was growing in the Lord by leaps and bounds, but her hubby was stuck in the concrete of unbelief. Then news came that they would be moving far away from our church. We continued to pray, and what God did still takes my breath away. Shortly after they moved, Michael, her husband, began building their new home. Becky started attending a church nearby, and the pastor began to pray for Michael and occasionally stopped by to visit. He was a bit of handyman himself, and soon he and a couple other men from church were helping Michael almost every day with his project. Then word came from Becky that Michael was attending church. Even though we had hated to lose Becky from our church, we could see that the Lord was using the move to bring about circumstances that might not have taken place here. Every so often when one of the two of us got discouraged, an email would arrive with new hope. Then in 2004 after Michael had back surgery, and a tornado destroyed their newly built garage and barn, Michael gave his life to the Lord. Praise His mighty name!

But whenever a man turns to the Lord, the veil is taken away. 2 Corinthians 3:16

Chapter 8 - Seek the God of the Impossible in Projects

The purpose of this chapter is to testify that whenever the Lord lays a particular project on your heart, you can know that He will be faithful to assist with all the details and resources for that event. When our desires line up with His, there is never a shortage of supply, even in our abilities. You may not be able to see how He will accomplish His purposes. The task may seem overwhelming, even impossible. But when God tugs on a person's heart to believe Him for something, He intends to accomplish it.

And God is able to make all grace abound to you, so that always having all sufficiency in everything, you may have an abundance for every good deed. 2 Corinthians 9:8

Now He who supplies seed to the sower and bread for food will supply and multiply your seed for sowing and increase the harvest of your righteousness; you will be enriched in everything for all liberality, which through us is producing thanksgiving to God. For the ministry of this service is not only fully supplying the needs of the saints, but is also overflowing through many thanksgivings to God. 2 Corinthians 9:10-12

In 2004, the Lord impressed us to host a Mother's Day Brunch. The purpose was to create opportunities to bring unsaved family members to church and over 300 people came to have brunch on the lawn of our church. Early in the planning stage, we realized that we would need some kind of shade for the day and began praying over this detail.

I checked into renting a big tent, but the cost would have been over four thousand dollars. It didn't take long to realize that this would not be good stewardship of the Lord's money even if we had that much to spend.

Day by day we asked the Lord for His will in the situation. We knew not many would enjoy food in our Southern California hundred-degree weather without shade. After weeks of praying, a friend of mine suggested using freestanding umbrellas and portable canopies, which seemed like a good idea at the time. However, we soon realized that forty-nine tables needed shade, while the sign up sheet showed that only four umbrellas and four canopies had been offered. We knew then that we would need help from the God of the Impossible. We didn't have money to just go out and rent or buy more and didn't think that even if we did, it would be a wise investment. Our church has very little storage space. I didn't know at the time if the Lord would change the weather or the umbrella situation, but we prayed.

Here's what the Lord did: First, our men's discipleship group saw us setting up and some of them offered to bring additional canopies from their homes. Second, in the course of grocery shopping, I ran into others from our church, and they offered umbrellas. Some drove by the church and saw the tables and umbrellas going up. They went home and brought more canopies and umbrellas. A friend went out and bought one of each to add to the supply. She had been my prayer partner over this whole shade request from the beginning. The next day during the church services, others saw tables still without shade and went home and got more umbrellas, so that by the time we ate there were only one or two tables without any shade, and these were not needed, so people moved to tables that did have shade.

We can limit our prayers by trying to figure out exactly how God is going to answer. If I had prayed, "God change the weather," I might have missed the blessing God had in mind. If I had said, "God please give us enough money to pay for a tent," I might have been disappointed. But we prayed, "God use the day to bring people to Christ and let the day be a tool for spiritual progress." Keep focusing on who God is and what His heart is for in every situation. He is always concerned about the salvation of people. He is big enough to figure out how to accomplish it. Present your needs to Him as we are told to do: *Be anxious for nothing, but in everything by prayer and supplication with thanksgiving let your requests be made known to*

God. Philippians 4:6 Trust Him to lead you in decision making along the way, and keep your spiritual eyes and ears open.

In 2004 we were asked to provide meals for our Vacation Bible School staff and their families for five nights. Our beginning budget for this endeavor was "0" and we ended up feeding 70-100 people each night. I remember placing this request on my prayer list and thinking, "Lord, if you don't provide this is really going to financially affect our vacation," which was scheduled for two weeks later. Each night we got to see the Lord work. He sent people with garden produce and toppings for our salad bar. He prompted another to donate ice for each night. One lady donated a turkey. Chick-Fil-A donated "nuggets" one night. He let one of our ladies discover a sale on ribs that saved lots of money. The meals were paid for with freewill offerings and at the end of the week the total cost not covered was only thirty-two cents. I considered that thirty-two cents a grand investment in the sixty-four who sought salvation that week. What a God we serve!

When God commissions a project He is there to see it to completion. Pray open, yet specific prayers. You might not know how God is going to answer, but be sure, He will answer. Ask Him to open up the resources to do His perfect will, even when there seems to be no hope.

Prayer journal entry:
4/21 Began praying for our children's camp, which will be held Aug. 27-29. Dean-o and the Dynamos will be ministering to our children.

8/12 Found out we have to pay for a minimum of 60 spaces for our children's camp. Only a few children are signed up. We asked the Lord to fill all spaces that He wanted filled.

8/20 There are twenty-five spaces filled so far. There are thirty-five left. We pray specifically that if there are children who are asking the Lord through their prayers to provide for their camp fees, that they will be able to attend.

8/22 Kids and Sunday School teachers washed approximately.

70 cars and earned over $1,000.

8/23 Donations of almost $800 were given towards scholarships.

8/24 All but three spaces have been filled. Praise the Lord!

8/25 Jeni, Stephanie and Rene, who work with our children ministries, called scholarship recipients. One little girl said, "God answered my prayer. I was asking God to help me go."

8/27 Sixty-two children and counselors attended camp. Eight gave their hearts to the Lord. It was a fantastic weekend for all of us.

On February 7, 2003, I prayed for God's help in planning a class I was teaching on hurt. One day as I was listening to the radio, I heard a song I felt would be a fantastic close to the class. At the time, I didn't have extra money to buy the CD, so I just kept it in prayer. After two weeks of praying, I finally got a check that could be put towards this venture. It was the actual day of the class. I went to a large Christian bookstore in our area. Unfortunately, they didn't have it in stock. So, I went to another bookstore in our area. The man in charge of the music didn't look hopeful when I asked for the title. He said, "I'm pretty sure we're out of that title, but I'll check for you." He returned smiling. "These came in and got put on the shelves and I didn't even know it!" The song was very effective in helping the students deal with the un-forgiveness that accompanies hurt and I have used it many times since then.

Prayer journal entry:

1/9/01 Prayed that the Lord would give us $5,000 to give to Empowering Lives International.

4/03 Our church had planned to take a missions trip with ELI, but because of unrest in the Congo, the trip was cancelled. The total raised for the trip, $9,100 was sent to help them with their work! Praise the Lord!

There have been many impossible things that I, and others, have prayed about for our church over the years. Recently, as I spent some time walking around our church property and praying, the Lord gave me a moment of realization: He had answered so many of these impossible requests, that I now needed to come up with new dreams to believe Him for. Here are just a few things the Lord pointed out that He had done for us:

-Our church property. (It is totally paid for.)

-Our church buildings. (One completed and two on the way.)

-Our bus ministry (We asked for a free bus and got it.)

-Our library and its resources (We asked for books, money to automate, and a bigger library and God gave them all.)

-The beautiful grounds and landscaping around our buildings. (God gave them to begin with, and Jeff, one of our staff members, loves to make them look beautiful. Together, they make a great team!)

-The playground equipment. (God gave us a beautiful fifty thousand dollar playground.)

-The bulletin boards that hang in each classroom. (Believe it or not, there was a time when these were needed, but there was no money to purchase them.)

-The mini-blinds on the windows. (Sunshine used to pour into Ike's office, as well as classrooms, and make work uncomfortable, so we prayed for these and the Lord provided—even though the budget money wasn't available for them at the time.)

-The $130,000 needed for our preschool modular. (This was recently paid off.)

-Additional space for our seventh grade. (We just had a new modular moved onto the property.)

-A bigger nursery was needed. (This was accomplished when we changed the functions of several rooms.)

One new dream: A place for anyone to pray—a garden with Scripture and beautiful plants that is accessible twenty-four hours a day. On our vacation we had a thought that kept us grinning. We visited a place in Jackson Hole, Wyoming that had a beautiful miniature golf course that looked like it could double as a prayer place. Since space is at a premium on our church property, we laughed about a dual usage prayer walk and miniature golf course: a prayer putt-putt. Smile. At the beginning of each hole there would be Scripture and subject ideas to get people started in their praying. Yes, I'm only kidding!

The realization of all the Jesus has done for us is overwhelming. I remember when our church didn't even own a typewriter! I remember when the only staff member was Ike. Now I read down a list of employee phone extensions that boggles my mind. Had we been given a glimpse of where our church is today when we were still packing it all up in the back of a trailer it would have been overwhelming. It is best just to see it accomplished one prayer request at a time.

Sometimes what God needs to meet a challenge is ability in you or someone else. This is the most difficult arena to believe Him for, in my opinion. There have been times over the years when we have watched a particular ministry leader used by God to lead a ministry in a way that seemed "beyond their abilities." Everyday we face our own inadequacies and we wonder, "How does the Lord use us?"

Moses must have understood. God had determined to bring His people through the wilderness. Moses' inability to "speak" was no obstacle for the One who made men's mouths. Perhaps the Lord has been calling you to a particular ministry challenge and you have been looking at your own resources or abilities. This will always result in feeling overwhelmed, like the ten spies felt when looking at giants in the Promised Land.

Make a decision today to focus on who God is and on His abilities. The one who flung several billion stars into place and who knows them each by name will have little difficulty equipping you for this new challenge. You don't have to see the path out of the wilderness to understand that He will bring you through it.

Prayer journal entry:
09/03 Asked the Lord for a gift of a certain amount to give His Nesting Place, a home for unwed mothers in Long Beach, California, at their annual fund-raising dinner. On the day before the event there was a financial gift of this very amount in my mail tray at the church office. It was a gift for Ike and me. I called and asked the one who

had given it for permission to use it for this purpose. The next day there was another gift. It was a donation from the same woman towards the banquet. She said she wanted it added to our gift. This gift doubled what I had asked the Lord for. Then we attended the banquet. Pastor Al Howard had a stirring message on "Giving the Precious." He had just participated in an extended fast and it was a powerful plea. The Lord reminded me that when there is something extremely critical, sometimes we charge the expense. He told me that saving the lives of the unborn qualified for this method of gift giving. Donations could be made by signing a commitment which we did. The gift I had initially asked for had been tripled by the time the Lord was done with it.

Not that we are adequate in ourselves to consider anything as coming from ourselves, but our adequacy is from God. 2 Corinthians 3:5

For I testify that according to their ability, and beyond their ability, they gave of their own accord, begging us with much urging for the favor of participation in the support of the saints, and this, not as we had expected, but they first gave themselves to the Lord and to us by the will of God. 2 Corinthians 8:3-5

'The Lord your God who goes before you will Himself fight on your behalf, just as He did for you in Egypt before your eyes, and in the wilderness where you saw how the Lord your God carried you, just as a man carries his son, in all the way which you have walked until you came to this place." Deuteronomy 1:30-31

Chapter 9 - Seek the God of the Impossible to Revive "Dead" Prayer Requests

Now in Joppa there was a certain disciple names Tabitha (which translated in Greek is called Dorcas); this woman was abounding with deeds of kindness and charity, which she continually did. And it came about at that time that she fell sick and died; and when they had washed her body, they laid it in an upper room. And since Lydda was near Joppa, the disciples, having heard that Peter was there, sent two men to him, entreating him, "Do not delay to come to us." And Peter arose and went with them. And when he had come, they brought him into the upper room; and all the widows stood beside him weeping, and showing all the tunics and garments that Dorcas used to make while she was with them. But Peter sent them all out and knelt down and prayed, and turning to the body, he said, "Tabitha, arise." And she opened her eyes, and when she saw Peter, she sat up. And he gave her his hand and raised her up; and calling the saints and widows, he presented her alive. And it became known all over Joppa and many believed in the Lord. Acts 9:36-42 translated in Greek is called Dorcas); this woman was abounding with deeds of kindness and charity, which she continually did. And it came about at that time that she fell sick and died; and when they had washed her body, they laid it in an upper room. And since Lydda was near Joppa, the disciples, having heard that Peter was there, sent two men to him, entreating him, "Do not delay to come to us." And Peter arose and went with them. And when he had come, they brought him into the upper room; and all the widows stood beside him weeping, and showing all the tunics and garments that Dorcas used to make while she was with them. But Peter sent them all out and knelt down and prayed, and turning to the body, he said, "Tabitha, arise." And she opened her eyes, and when she saw Peter, she sat up. And he gave her his hand and raised her up; and calling the saints and widows, he presented her alive. And it became known all over Joppa, and many believed in the Lord. Acts 9:36-42

God recently used this fascinating New Testament account to bless me. It was during my quiet time when He brought the following question to mind: Why did the two men entreat Peter to come? After all, Dorcus was already dead. Wasn't this prayer request "dead in the water?"

We have to ask ourselves, "Why do we pray about anything that seems impossible?" The answer must be, "Because of our faith in a God who does the impossible." My husband has a beautiful Scripture hanging on his office wall that was purchased by a friend of ours. It says, *"But He said, 'The things impossible with men are possible with God.'" Luke 18:27* Our God frequently does things that are totally impossible for men. Because of this, we must get used to asking for things that could not be done any other way. If men can accomplish it, it is no miracle. I like seeing the absolute impossible done through my prayers and this requires asking God to do things no man can do.

Just prior to this New Testament account Peter healed a man named Aeneas. *Peter said to him, "Aeneas, Jesus Christ heals you; get up and make your bed." Immediately he got up. Acts 9:34* He had been paralyzed for eight years. That's a long time for someone to be out of commission. Yet the next day, he was out and about his city in perfect health. In another New Testament account, a woman, bent over with a demon, was made to walk upright in an instant after eighteen years of suffering. A man born blind was cured after forty years. God is in the business of doing incredible things.

So as these two men watched their friend Dorcus die and sat through the sorrowful preparations for a funeral, they decided that there was still hope. They got off their seats, out of their comfort zone and started searching for a man named Peter, whom they had learned had been used by God to heal. There were plenty of people back at the house still crying and mourning, but two men believed and it made all the difference.

It's similar to when the Israelites entered the Promised Land. Two believing men stood out in a crowd of weepers and wailers. Friend, when everything looks bleak around you, are you one who looks up to the God of the Impossible and begins to believe, or do you hang out with the criers, the whiners and the mourners?

Have you heard the joke that begins, "How many psychologists does it take to change a light bulb?" The answer is, "Only one, but the light bulb really has to want to change." Here's a question to think on today: "How many people does it take to do a miracle?" The answer is, "Two, but one of them has to be the Son of God." It is important for us to remember in our praying that we are connected to Almighty God in our prayer work. What man could never think of doing is child's play for our God. Instead of wondering why these two men believed God to raise their dead friend, we should be asking ourselves, "Why don't I choose more often to believe God will answer seemingly dead prayer requests?"

Why is it considered incredible among you people if God does raise the dead? Acts 26:8

There is another miracle hidden in the depths of this passage and in the life of this woman. The Scripture says, *"This woman was abounding with deeds of kindness and charity, which she continually did."* Think about this: one woman lived out a life that abounded with deeds of kindness and charity. Anyone who has been used by God to do something extraordinary knows two things that are required: time and money. To take flowers to a shut in, or to make a meal for a sick person, you must dedicate some time and some resources. But here is a woman who was continually doing loving things for others around her. This is a miracle that cannot be overlooked. She had discovered a well of resource.

She had found her vine/branch relationship with the Almighty to be an open door to the well of kindness. It's from the heart that our words and deeds spring forth. At the source of her work was not a low self esteem or need to please. Dorcas gave because she cared. She saw needs around her, but instead of recoiling to safety and self indulgence, her heart of love compelled her to action. This same kindness must have been what propelled Peter and John when they encountered the lame man in Acts chapter three. You see, the real miracle in the passage is that one woman realized that the team of God and Dorcus could touch any situation with love and good deeds, and that there was no situation that could not be softened and saturated with God's power, if she was willing to believe. The Bible says that she continually did this. It was the mark of her life and the root of her reputation.

...having a reputation for good works; and if she has brought up children, if she has shown hospitality to strangers, if she has washed the saints' feet, if she has assisted those in distress, and if she has devoted herself to every good work. 1 Timothy 5:10

For if the readiness is present, it is acceptable according to what a person has, not according to what he does not have. 2 Corinthians 8:12

In the process of loving, Dorcus must have also learned that God means it when He promises all that we need to fulfill every desire for goodness. *2 Thessalonians 1:11 To this end also we pray for you always that our God may count you worthy of your calling, and fulfill every desire for goodness and the work of faith with power.* This is such an important principle in our praying. There is no desire of our hearts, no unvoiced prayer that God can't fulfill. There is no seed of faith that He can't use to grow something good for His kingdom and His people. So start living on the scale that Dorcus did. Start allowing God to make your opportunities abound in spreading kindness and charity. Trust Him to fill your life with the necessary time and resources to accomplish the impossible and start rejoicing, because God will certainly grow a garden out of the little faith seeds you plant in your heart today.

Prayer journal entry:

June 2004: Asked God to replace resources that I had used for several projects He had called me to do. These projects had left our family's checking account "low." June 15, 2004: In one day he restored all the money used for three areas of ministry.

Prayer journal entry:

July 2004: God asked me to give away a birthday gift I had received to someone who needed it more than I did. The next week He gave me another gift which was more than five times the amount of the original gift that had been sacrificed.

I have two friends who live like Dorcus did. They look like ordinary people on the outside. But inside they are big dreamers for God. I think they must take His breath away at times with their great faith. They have God businesses. Their goal in life is to live on ten percent of what they make and give God the other ninety percent. That takes faith. But God is blessing them in an incredible way. Their lives stand out like beacon lights in a world focused on self as a giant billboard to the Living God who changes hearts, and I know they make Him smile.

Do you make God smile by your prayer requests? Have you ever taken His breath away with your faith? Start living like Dorcus! I think that's why her two friends believed that even though she was dead, she needed to live again. There was too much work and ministry to be done and they needed someone who understood the God of Resource to accomplish it. Her friends had been affected by her great faith living. So instead of wringing their hands and giving up on their faithful friend, they might have thought, "What would Dorcus do if she were here?" That might have prompted them to say, "She would believe God." Even when everything looked washed up and impossible, Dorcus would always say, "God can make a way." So they just had to believe. They had to go to Joppa and start looking for the man called Peter whom they had heard about.

God could have said no to their request. As a matter of fact, Peter could have said no to their request. Peter could have been too preoccupied with his work to come. But we know that's not what happened because Peter had learned to operate at the direction of the Spirit of the Lord. His prayer life had changed and grown and decisions were not made in the flesh any longer. Not only did the two men believe God for a miracle, but Peter did as well. He began to pray. How long did he pray? We don't know, but we do know this: God responded yes to their prayer. One interesting description about their request is that they entreated Peter to come. I had the privilege of doing a word study on this term, which is used in connection with many accounts of miracles in the New Testament. The word means to beg or implore. Usually when this particular word is chosen, someone decides they are going to press in to receive an answer. It involves tenacity along with a heart attitude of humility and a plea for mercy. What was the result? No one who entreated was ever turned away. I am not implying that if you beg God you won't ever receive no as an answer, just that it is an arena of asking that many seldom experience.

There are times we don't know the best way to pray in a situation, but as long as we are entreating the Lord, as long as we are begging Him to act on the situation, we can be assured that He will. We will not be left empty-handed in our praying. When we look up from our circumstances, we will find ourselves holding onto His perfect will and this is never disappointing to us.

Peter had to be a man of faith or he wouldn't have prayed for Aeneas, the paralytic, who had been bedridden for eight years. If you're going to pray over things that have looked impossible for eight years, you are going to have to have a well of faith/hope, which is found in the Holy Spirit.

Four years ago my friend Marilyn requested prayer for an extended family member whose husband was into the occult, and was influencing his wife and their three children. I just received a report that this young woman is now saved and attending a regular Bible study. Praise the God who can answer "impossible" prayer requests.

And Jesus answered and said to them, "Truly I say to you, if you have faith, and do not doubt, you shall not only do what was done to the fig tree, but even if you say to this mountain, 'Be taken up and cast into the sea,' it shall happen." Matthew 21:21

Last fall we had a faith pledge drive for our school. I had been the one to challenge our families to ask God for something to give to our embryonic jr. high. At the time our family had nothing to give beyond our regular tithes and offerings, but in faith we had asked the Lord to give us a huge amount. We were committed that if the Lord gave our family this amount that it would be set aside for this work. Just months after making that pledge, we watched the Lord fulfill it. It almost took my breath away to write the check. God had once again answered an impossible prayer request with abundance.

We were having a rash of cancer victims in our church during the year of 2004. My friend, Renee, whom I mentioned earlier, had been healed of cancer eight years ago, but had just been told that the cancer had again invaded her body. This was difficult to understand. Renee had been so close to death before, but the Lord had radically helped her. This had brought her and her family to the Lord and had resulted in much progress for the kingdom. So when she was told that she had just months to live, it threw all of us for a loop. Renee had cancer scares every few years, usually at the time of Vacation Bible School. We think this was a result of her leadership of this program at our church. Something would show up on her yearly physical exam. The church would rally to prayer, and miraculously, the spot or tests would clear. When Renee was again told that her body was full of devastating cancer, we went to war. She had received the news right before our women's retreat. During the retreat, she had shared with all our ladies there that she was ready to die if that was the Lord's will. Much prayer was made on her behalf, and weeks later she received a second opinion that was radically different from the one she had initially received. This one brought hope and although she still had cancer, the treatment and timeline were a world apart from what she had been told initially. Once again, we had seen God do the impossible. We are still praying for a complete healing, but we rejoice in the different "verdict" she now has from the medical field.

There are plenty of people to weep over prayer requests that have been dead or unmovable for years. But God's not looking for mourners, but believers. It takes big faith to believe for big things. That's why there are not a lot of people doing it. Smile.

In 2004, our women's ministry leader decided that no woman who wanted to attend retreat should be held back by a limit on finances. This meant believing for a huge amount of scholarships. After all the gifts had been given, Kim realized that she still needed five hundred and fifteen dollars to pay off the scholarship expenses. As incredible as it seems, one final offering taken for scholarships resulted in a total of exactly five hundred and fifteen dollars! What a wonderful response the Lord gave Kim's faith!

I heard one time that in fund raising, if you ask a little gift of a big donor, that you can actually offend them. Are you offending God by little prayers? Are your prayers allowing God to live up to His potential? Do your prayer requests tap into the desires God has for setting captives free, raising the dead, healing the sick and spreading the gospel?

Truly, truly, I say to you, he who believes in Me, the works that I do shall he do also; and greater works than these shall he do; because I go to the Father. John 14:12

If you can accomplish a task by yourself with your own resources, then it's not faith that you're employing to accomplish it. Many times right before a big project I find that finances are tight. Oh there's always money for food and house payments, but not enough to pay for my own manufactured miracles. I believe God does this for a reason. It's more difficult to know God's will when you can just write a check and handle a situation (in the flesh). It takes His part of the bargain to steer our decision making, and when our resources are limited and He opens the door of supply, it's much easier to tell what He's saying.

Through a number of circumstances, the Lord led our church to partner with another church in town to raise money for a ministry called God's Kitchen. This ministry began by another "Dorcus." Her name is Betty Schultz. Back in 1984, Betty started feeding the poor through the kitchen of her church, Corona First Baptist Church. Here in her words is what the Lord did and continues to do through her obedience and faith:

In 1984, dinners were served one night a week. Then, in 1986, dinners were served two nights a week. In 1989, the ministry was expanded to five nights a week, with many other churches volunteering on a regular basis to prepare and serve dinner.

In October 1995, The Circle of Hope Shelter opened, and the feeding program moved to the shelter and expanded again to three meals a day, seven days a week. More churches joined in the endeavor.

We presently have over 20 churches committed to cooking and serving at least one day per month. Many other churches are represented with one or more volunteers working when possible. In 2003, we served over 10,000 breakfasts, 9,500 lunches (with 6,000 of the lunches being sack lunches for children living on the street and workers in the Transitional Program), and 41,400 dinners bringing our total meals to over 61,000. Volunteers put in 13,500 hours of volunteer time. Since moving to the shelter location in 1995, we have served over 560,000 meals. Since our beginnings in 1984, we have served well over one million free meals.

Wow! Now that kind of work requires faith! Betty obviously has found the well of resources and has connected to it. So when two churches wanted to do something for Betty and her ministry, we needed to show some faith also. Corona Evangelical Free Church offered to bring their 60-voice choir and 27-piece orchestra to perform a concert of Great Anthems of the Church as a benefit for this wonderful cause. After we had made the arrangements, I found out that their concert really centered on the piano and their fine pianist. We have only had digital keyboards at our church, and it just seemed fitting that we should have a piano to use for the evening, so we began to pray. We had our own instrumentalists begin praying for a grand piano. I called a piano store whose ad I saw in a flyer. I had no idea that this was a Christian operated business and that the owner Francisco was a committed Christian. I simply faxed our request for a grand piano and waited for an answer. Just days before the concert, we received word that he would donate a baby grand for the occasion. What a miracle! That was exciting, but it wasn't all God had in store for that evening. Our local Christian radio station, KSGN, was so gracious! They put our event on their web page and even had each announcer make an announcement over the air. The Lord was "on our side." He loves the poor, and when our hearts are genuinely tenderized to do something for them, we usually have His support and resources.

The concert was such a kick in the enemy's face. Many churches came together to enjoy beautiful music. That was the second miracle. Then it was time for the offering. (I had asked God for one thousand dollars. I was delighted because our counters came up with twenty-three hundred dollars.) But then Pastor Hegg from Evangelical Free Church added a gift from their body, and over three thousand dollars was raised for God's Kitchen. More gifts came in even after the evening was over. Praise God who can do what we cannot!

Here is a question to think on: What did Dorcus do after she was resuscitated from the dead? I'm sure she made more garments. I'm sure she did more deeds of kindness and charity. But now that she knew that even death must obey the command of the Lord, there would have been no stopping her.

Sometimes what stops God's hand is our own human minds deciding that what we have asked for is out of reach and too difficult for God. When there is no hope in the physical what do you do? This is the time to pray seemingly impossible prayers.

When Eutychus fell out the window during Paul's lengthy sermon in Acts chapter twenty and was dead on arrival, they didn't call 911 or the mortuary. Paul embraced the situation and the young man, with prayer. (This is understood, though not specifically stated in the passage) and his life was restored. That was an impossible situation. But his family got him back alive and whole that night because God can do anything He wants. Human reasoning would have halted that prayer before it ever got started.

I know there are situations in your life where something just seems too sad, just too awful to be right. It's then that our praying must begin, not end. It's when all human possibilities fail that faith moves in and compels us to believe.

We see the Old Testament Israelites outnumbered so many times. They were surrounded by the enemy and basically marked for death, either through war or starvation. They cried out to the living God, and miraculously, the enemy turned to fight each other, or run away, or fall down dead. Today the enemy may have your family by the throat. He might have your resources surrounded, but a prayer of faith can send him running. Believe God for what He can do and not what you can do. Trust Him today, and pray for what only the true and living, Almighty and powerful God can answer.

If you received all that you prayed about today, what would you get? Would you find life for someone who's dead? Would the kingdom of God have more resources? Would someone be healed by your prayer today? If not, the problem in praying is you. You are limiting what God wants to do. Pray extravagant prayers and see them answered. Of course, God can say no to some of those prayers. That's because He knows best. But how many opportunities are you giving Him to do the impossible?

Lazarus, Eutychus (Acts 20:9) and Dorcus had something in common. The enemy had tried to declare death over them, but God had declared life over them. Can you imagine their testimonies? Their lives would have been magnetized because they witnessed the resurrection power of Christ firsthand. When you start praying impossible prayers that get answered, you too will find your life magnetized by the resurrection power that brings others to believe.

Note: Peter, Paul and Jesus are the ones in these specific Bible situations who show us that the circumstances we are in are not necessarily what God wants for us. A corpse isn't always an indication of that person's immediate future when God is in charge. Sometimes coffins get turned into planter boxes just because that's the way He wants it to be. So look around for things the enemy has nailed up and started to bury. Start uncovering hope for those you love and make a difference in the kingdom.

My current seemingly impossible prayer request list:
1. Cancer victim to be healed.
2. Leukemia victim to be healed. (Our friend Gary passed away as the book was being written.)
3. Revival in Corona.
4. Salvation of hard-core loved ones.
5. Ike's health to be restored.
6. Friend who has suffered panic attacks for over a year to be healed. (Prayer journal said on 12/28/02 this friend asked for help. On July 4, 2004, she was finally able to attend church again and receive the encouragement of the morning service. We are still believing for a complete recovery)
7. The Lord to give our church the land from the youth building to the freeway.
8. The Lord to give our church the houses along Rudell Road to be used for housing for unwed mothers, a retirement home for Christian workers, more space for our food panty, clothing ministry, a home for alcoholic rehabilitation, a bookstore, a more extensive library, etc.
9. Our sanctuary to be filled at Morning Prayer.

There is one other theme of this passage that we should not overlook. It is the fact that two men went off to find Peter. It took two to begin this miracle. It is so very important to have prayer partners that you pray with regularly. One alone can get discouraged, but two together can believe God for anything. We all need someone to hear us pray impossible prayers, so that when they become a reality, we have witnesses!

Praise: Several years ago at our church's women's retreat, my friend, Deena, voiced a prayer that we would develop prayer partners as a church. This past retreat showed the fulfillment of that prayer as many of the women took up the challenge and began praying in groups of two.

Again I say to you, that if two of you agree on earth about anything that they may ask, it shall be done for them by My Father who is in heaven. For where two or three have gathered together in My name, there I am in their midst. Matthew 18:19-20

Chapter 10 - Get Power Through Corporate Prayer

In 2004, the Lord began to take our congregation deeper into the realm of corporate prayer. We had been meeting weekly in the morning and in the evening, and regularly before/during services. Then one of our prayer warriors felt that we should begin praying every morning at the church, as well as in our own individual prayer times. This seemed to match with what the Lord had been saying through my husband's messages on revival so we began a new adventure. Almost immediately we began to see two things change: the power and effectiveness of ministry and the intensity of our daily schedules seemed to double. The first change was obviously God's response to our hungering for more time in His presence. The second seemed to be the enemy's response to our offensive strategies.

Three weeks after this daily prayer time began, one of our devoted prayer warriors mentioned that the Lord had given him an analogy for this new commitment of time: our new found power in corporate prayer was like a trampoline—it was the means of gaining heightened progress in our ministries. Another outcome we began to enjoy was the teamwork that God used when we met together to pray.

One morning I came into prayer with a personal daily agenda that could have filled two days. But as a result of praying together, the Lord pricked my heart to instead offer help to one of our children's ministry directors. Jeni was preparing for a big outreach concert and was going to sort and package two hundred Vacation Bible School T-shirts and registration materials into packets that day. When we looked at what needed to be done, we realized that it was a huge project. I left our time of prayer and made a few quick God-directed phone calls from the church office. An hour later we had around ten workers busily sorting, folding and wrapping. The project took all of us several hours to complete. We realized later that Jeni could never have done it by herself in one day like she had planned. The Lord knew that, and He used our corporate prayer time to unite us to complete His work.

The Lord had also used the prayer time to alert us about getting the event on the radio and after completing the work project, I drove straight to the radio station with some CDs to be given away. They graciously announced the concert and the Lord blessed our time with the group God Rocks. The concert was a huge success with many children praying for salvation and rededicating their lives to Christ. Without that corporate prayer time God's work would have been severely hindered. Through prayer, hearts, minds, resources and focus were concentrated where God wanted it that day.

We have seen many examples of this same effect since we began to pray together in this way. When we pray corporately there is no set agenda. The Lord brings up the topics He wants prayed over and how He wants us to pray through those that are there that day. The results are the very thing we need that day.

One of our favorite invitations during prayer is to ask the Lord to pray His heart through us. Then, as we pray, it is interesting to see that various topics that the Lord brings up. Sometimes the things He lays on our hearts seem too big for us to have thought up.

We have also seen interesting and powerful things take place in the first few moments following corporate prayer. Details are communicated that help avoid ministry collisions like double use of facilities or equipment. Also, enthusiasm for projects moves quickly throughout the different ministry areas, creating a bond and support that often doubles the effectiveness of the event.

One day I arrived at prayer with a heavy agenda. A funeral was being held that day and I needed to buy my husband a white shirt, finish a visual presentation for the service, rehearse the music and prepare the food for the family following the service. I also had a worship team rehearsal for the service that evening and the service itself. As we ended our time of prayer my friend Karie asked if there was anything I needed help with. When I mentioned the white shirt she said that she could easily pick one up as she shopped that morning. In addition she and her daughter, Sondra, came back to help with preparing and serving the dinner. If they hadn't done these things, I know that I wouldn't have made it. I saw that without their help and the help of others, we never would have had the meal ready on time. What was impossible on my part became possible through the answers of corporate prayer.

How I wish I could communicate this message to others in our church! If they could experience the sharpening of weapons, the stockpiling of resources and the aiming of grenades, they would see the necessity of coming together each day so that the Holy Spirit can get us all tuned to the same wavelength. There is nothing better than corporate prayer to get everyone in a church on the same page. I realize this is why the mission trips of Paul and Barnabas were so successful. They began with united prayer. If there is one goal I have for our church this year, it is to communicate this principle and to encourage all our staff members to pray with each other before they begin their "normal work day."

We have also seen the Lord grow other times of corporate prayer throughout our church body. A Saturday men's group has spent valuable time praying together. The youth leadership has seen a change in the amount of time they spend together in prayer.

This has produced a "soothing" effect on the spiritual warfare attacks aimed by the enemy. Previously he could get two people unhappy with each other resulting in division and strife; however, as a direct outcome of more corporate prayer, we see the added power of conflict resolution. Lives that the enemy has derailed because of personal hurt have gotten back on track resulting in service and growth. This can only be attributed to a greater effectiveness in discernment, communication and strategy. All these result from our times of corporate prayer. (A commitment to corporate prayer does not guarantee fewer challenges. Sometimes prayer is what stirs them up.)

Entering the arena of corporate prayer is not without pitfalls. Greater praying may result in more ways that the enemy can try to work. I have much to learn about corporate prayer, but I have already seen some ways the enemy has tried to discourage our praying together:

1. Getting prayer warriors praying in a different fashion.
2. Distractions occurring during corporate prayer.
3. Getting those praying distracted with too many subjects or no peaceful resolution in the prayers. This is where we jump from one topic to another, but never get to "pray through" on any of them. This results in a feeling of disconcertedness when leaving the place of prayer.
4. Having one person dominating the prayer time and not allowing others to pray, as they wanted. Sometimes I am the person the Lord has corrected.

We are learning much about this venue of prayer, but one thing we know: We would never want to go back to our former prayer experience. Knowing what the Lord has done in response to our hunger for Him has shown us that we can never be disappointed with more prayer.

Where is your church in the place of corporate prayer? Is the Lord calling you to begin this area of ministry? It is not easy to get over the initial hurdle of having more than one or two people praying together regularly. The enemy hates it and will fight hard as you begin. But there is nothing that will nurture God's church and His people better and faster than corporate prayer. So, just do it.

And when he realized this, he went to the house of Mary, the mother of John who was also called Mark, where many were gathered together and were praying. Acts 12:12

And on the Sabbath day we went outside the gate to a riverside, where we were supposing that there would be a place of prayer; and we sat down and began speaking to the women who had assembled. Acts 16:13

Chapter 11 - Realize a Double Portion of the Spirit of God

If you then, being evil, know how to give good gifts to your children, how much more shall your heavenly Father give the Holy Spirit to those who ask Him? Luke 11:13

In 2 Kings 2, we read of a wonderful encounter between Elijah and Elisha. Elisha has been in training under the ministry of Elijah ever since he began the prestigious job of washing Elijah's hands (2 Kings 3:11). He has seen the mighty miracles by God through this prophet, and the personal integrity of a true man of God. When the last moments of Elijah's life come, he asks, "Elisha, do you have any final prayer requests?" Elisha responds immediately, "I want a double portion of the Spirit that's at work in you."

It is important to note that the "spirit of Elijah" is really a phrase to denote the work of God's Spirit in a human being's life. Elisha is not saying, "I want to be like Elijah." He is saying, "I want to be filled with the Spirit of God like Elijah."

There are many people who desire the power of God in their lives. Simon, the sorcerer, when he saw the miracles done through Philip, wanted the power of God. Simon had been a man of authority who had been at the center of the attention in his town. When he saw the work of the Holy Spirit, he wanted it so badly that he offered a bribe. (Acts 8:9-24)

You can't walk in the Spirit of God and your own flesh at the same time. If you want God's Spirit, even a single portion, you must give up self. Great power comes with great yielded-ness.

When I make homemade bread I use one and a quarter cups of liquid. Usually it is water. I also use two tablespoons of oil. However, when I make homemade rolls, I want richer dough, so I use milk for the liquid and butter for the shortening. The texture of the roll dough is so much better than that required for bread. Sometimes the ingredients I use are limited by what I have on hand. Any combination will do, but the better the ingredients, the better the product. It is like this in our lives. The more water and oil, representing us, that we take out of the measuring cup, the more room that's available for the butter and milk, the good stuff representing His Spirit. You can't have it both ways. You must give up one for the other. John the Baptist understood this concept and said, *"...Less of me and more of Him."*

Empty Me [3]
Holy fire burn away
My desire for anything
That is not of You
But is of me
I want more of You
And less of me
Empty me
Empty me
Fill in me
With You, with You

The day Elijah was taken up to Heaven, Elisha made some costly choices. Elijah was told by God to go to Gilgal, then Bethel and then beyond the Jordan. Each time he let Elisha know that he could do whatever he wanted to do. But Elisha declared each time that he was sticking with Elijah. He knew that Elijah was being taken to Heaven that day and he didn't want to miss the experience. All in all, if you study your Bible map, their journey that day was a pretty healthy walk, over twenty miles. In those days being a prophet cost something. It would have been easier that day to have stayed home and been a couch potato. But Elisha wanted to be ready for God's blessing and on this particular day that meant that he had to be available, even though it wasn't easy to do so.

When Elijah was finally taken up, Elisha witnessed this incredible encounter between Heaven and earth. And, most importantly, he received God's answer to his prayer request for more of the Spirit.

Elisha had proven by his life that day that he was willing to pay the cost of being doubly used by God. He was willing to "go the extra mile" that is sometimes required to be greatly used by God, and as a result, he received the blessing of that decision. All around us are those who are content with the rewards of this world. But we can be encouraged that when our greatest desire becomes being filled with more of God's Spirit, His response is always yes. When we make room by moving away from our self-seeking ambitions, He is sure to fill the space with a greater capacity for His power and love.

The more God's Spirit is at work in our lives, the more wisdom we have available to make right choices. Because God's Spirit is God Himself, it means that His presence in our lives gives us a greater capacity to create. Remember when men were chosen to build the Tabernacle? The character quality at the top of the list was the Spirit of God. With God's Spirit at work in the workman's life, God could teach him what He wanted done and how.

And I have filled him with the Spirit of God in wisdom, in understanding, in knowledge, and in all kinds of craftsmanship. Exodus 31:3

It is the same for us. If we want to know how to raise godly children, have a happy marriage and lead effective ministries, what we need more than anything else is a double portion of God's Spirit within us.

God showed David how the temple was to be constructed. He said in 1 Chronicles 29:18 that God wrote all the details of the pattern for construction on his heart. *1 Chronicles 28:19 "All this," said David, "the Lord made me understand in writing by His hand upon me, all the details of this pattern."*

This is an important concept because we are told that the earthly temple was based on a heavenly structure. How could David know what was in heaven? How could he know how to place the furniture inside that would create the pattern of the cross, table of showbread, menorah, mercy seat, ark of the covenant, cherubim, etc.? It was impossible without the Holy Spirit. But impossible tasks become simple when the mind of Almighty God is at work within us. Therefore, there is nothing greater to seek than more of His Spirit in our lives and ministries.

However, the Lord will be watching the choices we make, just as He watched Elisha. Are we willing to lay down temporal pleasures to aim for those that are eternal? Are we willing to clear our schedules for more time in His presence or are we content to pass the time in trivial pursuits? This will determine how much of us will be available for Him to fill.

I led music for a retreat one day where the speaker prayed a simple prayer for a friend of mine. "More," he prayed. He was asking for more of the Holy Spirit to fall on him. Suddenly my friend fell to the ground under a genuine touch of God on his body. The speaker had been quick to tell us that he had not touched or pushed my friend at all. This is the kind of experience most Christians are looking for. They just want God's Spirit to "fall on them" and sometimes it does.

I love the story of two Free Methodist ladies who sat on the front pew in D. L. Moody's meetings and prayed that the Holy Spirit would "fall on him." When he noticed their prayers and asked what they were praying about, he became a little irritated to find that they were praying for him (as opposed to the unsaved.) But later, he joined them in their prayer, and it wasn't too long afterward that walking through town, Moody felt the Spirit of God touch him mightily and he had to stop at the house of a friend and request a room in which to get away with God. After this point in time he said his preaching was never the same. There was never a meeting where someone didn't accept Christ, and there was new power that he had never known before.

But whether God's Spirit simply falls on you, or whether, through choices of obedience, He finds more room to work in your life, one thing is certain, we need more of Him.

In these last days we are promised that His Spirit will fall on both male and female servants. So let us come boldly into the throne room of God and ask for more. Today, get away from the hustle and bustle of your city, as D. L. Moody did, and allow the touch of God to change your will and your work.

It was God's Spirit who helped Paul recognize the evil intentions behind Simon's pious request (Acts 8:21) and it is God's Spirit that will declare the thoughts and intentions of a man's heart, so that he recognizes the work of God among us. So what are we waiting for? Let's ask for more.

I love the way Jesus lets us know how He feels about such a request. He is telling us plainly that asking for more of His Spirit is a good request and that His response will always be yes to this request.

And I say to you, ask, and it shall be given to you; seek, and you shall find; knock, and it shall be opened to you. For everyone who asks, receives; and he who seeks, finds; and to him who knocks, it shall be opened. Now suppose one of you fathers is asked by his son for a fish; he will not give him a snake instead of a fish, will he? Or if he is asked for an egg, he will not give him a scorpion, will he? If you then, being evil, know how to give good gifts to your children, how much more shall your heavenly Father give the Holy Spirit to those who ask Him? Luke 11:9-13

In one day my kids asked for three things I had no intention of ever giving them. They wanted ice cream cones right before dinner. They wanted a pet fish (we had been through that before and found I was the only one to feed it). And they wanted another cat (we already had two). I remember telling them, "Ask me for something I want to give you. I like to give you things you need. But I have no intention of giving you ice cream right before supper or a fish or another cat." It's the same way with God. If we're not seeing our prayers answered, we might be asking for things He knows aren't good for us or things He has no intention of granting us. But if our requests line up with something we know He wants to give us, He will grant the request we have made of Him.

In the Luke passage we read earlier, God is clearly telling us that He loves giving good gifts and that one gift He loves giving is more of His Spirit in our lives. So start asking for what God is just waiting to give you—more power, more effectiveness, more love—more of Himself. You won't get stuck with a snake or a scorpion, like a white elephant gift at a party. You'll get exactly what you ask for, so turn aside today and every day with this sincere request. Keep asking and you'll keep receiving. Keep seeking and you'll keep finding. Keep knocking and the door will keep being opened unto you.

Choices affect God's ability to grant this request

If you want more of the Lord's Spirit to dwell in you, you will find yourself having to leave the presence of sin. God's Spirit is grieved by sin and this directly affects your ability to endure it.

One time I was the guest at a dinner in a restaurant where the entertainment quickly turned to what I felt was debauchery. I was a passenger in someone else's car and thought I had no discreet means of escape. The next morning in my quiet time, I could feel the Lord was angry. I tried using this flimsy excuse, "I couldn't leave, Lord. I didn't have a car." It went over about as well as Aaron telling God he just threw in the gold and out came a calf. I felt the Lord saying that if I had pointed out the need to leave, that we would have all left. I had been a wimpy leader in these off-duty moments. The journey with God requires giving up other things, which include, among other things, the affirmation of others. On several occasions the Lord has shown me that I can't please Him if I choose to please others. The shame of these moments helps me choose better the next time I am faced with the challenge.

Another choice that will need to be made, if you are to be a vessel of God's Holy Spirit, will be to respond to a higher calling and the responsibilities of a higher Kingdom. It is so easy to become involved with the day-to-day affairs of this life. So easy, as a matter of fact, that it will take very little thought not to become caught up in the traffic on this highway of behavior. However, for those who want a double portion of God's Spirit, there will need to turn away from the affairs of this world in order to concentrate on those of the next one. This will cost time and attention, but it will be amply repaid with blessings in the spirit realm.

No soldier in active service entangles himself in the affairs of everyday life, so that he may please the one who enlisted him as a soldier. 2 Timothy 2:4

When the Lord pressed in on us to begin praying together at our church each morning we found that there were sacrifices to be made. This meant setting aside time every morning to attend. It also required gas to get to the church and other hidden costs, such as giving up valuable morning writing time, etc. But the Lord was so good. He made it feel like there were more hours in the day. Tasks went smoother and quicker than I had expected. He brought the treasure of His presence and the reward of answered prayers. I definitely got the bargain in the deal. Smile. When you exchange the pressing and urgent demands of the ordinary in order to respond to the heavenly call, you too will find that the rewards are out of this world.

One final decision that will affect God's ability to fill you in a greater way is your tolerance of your own personal sin. If you are going to go deeper with the Lord, you will find that sin or even "relational flack"[4] cannot be tolerated. As soon as the sin is made known to you, you must confess and be brought back into right relationship. I am not saying that any Christian should allow the presence of sin in their lives, but what I am saying is that the more God is using you, the less He will put up with stubbornness and pride.

If the Lord sees you, in the quiet moments of your heart, responding to His pricking immediately and wholeheartedly, He can't help Himself. He will respond to your desire for more and grant you a deeper revelation of Himself. So in essence, you determine how much of God's Spirit can be at work in you.

Think of how the Lord used the apostle Paul. Even handkerchiefs that he had touched were laid on the sick and they were healed. But this kind of usage took Paul deeper in prayer, deeper in sacrifice, deeper in dependence, deeper in obedience and deeper in self-control. As you make choices today about how you will spend your time, money and attention, consider what the Lord did through the lives of those who went farther on in obedience with Him. Leave the company of those bent on sinning. Set your sights on a heavenly standard and rid your heart of any known sin or doubtful habit. You too will experience a greater capacity to contain the magnificent Spirit of God and to be used in His service.

Chapter 12 - Enroll in the School of Fasting

In your journey of prayer, the school of fasting will need to become a regular activity. Fasting heightens our effectiveness in prayer. It opens our awareness to our neediness. Fasting can mean giving up food or some other treasured pleasure for a time in order to devote more time for prayer. [5] As a person who really enjoys food, fasting has been difficult for me over the years. I used to "hate" it, and resented God calling me to do it. But now, even though it is still a challenge, I look forward to the times when God allows me to "feast" on deeper things with Him. It has been quite a journey, and I'd like to share some of the process with you. Hopefully, it will encourage you in this area.

One of my most vivid first encounters with fasting came at an event we didn't even plan. We were invited to attend a three-day prayer convention, at a friend's expense, in Los Angeles. We didn't find out until it began that fasting was a part of the plan and that meals were not included. Smile. Conventions in my mind just go together with eating. When an entire day of intense prayer was over and we headed back to the hotel room, I was thoroughly exhausted. All I could think about was food. Somehow, we managed to make it through the night with a banquet of bottled water, and the next morning enjoyed another great session of corporate prayer. We are so trained to think about food—like clockwork, three times a day. As the time wore on I felt I couldn't make it through the day without eating. I somehow, like Eve, convinced my husband that we needed to eat. We ended up walking several city blocks in search of food.

As I look back, it's easy to see that the Lord was trying to help us not eat. There just weren't any places open within this area of the city. We spotted one place and stopped inside, but the prices were too high. After we had left and walked another couple of blocks, I realized that I had left my purse back there, and we had to retrace our steps. Now, the memory seems humorous. The Lord was doing everything to help us keep our commitment to Him. But I was determined to eat. After walking block after block, we finally found a place and sat down to eat.

As soon as the food hit my mouth, I felt like the Israelites probably did after their dinner of quail.[6] I felt ashamed. I knew I had disappointed the Lord and had influenced my husband to do wrong, not right. After a time of true repentance, the Lord used that horrible "taste in my mouth" to help me learn some things about fasting. I decided that I would never again agree to fast and wimp out. The recollection of how the shame felt helps me keep my commitments, no matter how difficult. I'm sure the Apostle Peter would be able to relate with this conversation.

There are many reasons to fast. Fasting stockpiles our spiritual resources. It helps clear our spiritual vision. It breaks down barriers in hearts and minds. And it opens the spiritual pores to receive a fresh touch from God.

Some instructions from the Lord on making your fast effective:

"Why have we fasted and Thou dost not see? Why have we humbled ourselves and Thou dost not notice?" "Behold, on the day of your fast you find your desire, and drive hard all your workers. Behold, you fast for contention and strife and to strike with a wicked fist. You do not fast like you do today to make your voice heard on high. Is it a fast like this which I choose, a day for a man to humble himself? Is it for bowing one's head like a reed, and for spreading out sackcloth and ashes as a bed? Will you call this a fast, even an acceptable day to the Lord? Is this not the fast which I choose, to loosen the bonds of wickedness, to undo the bands of the yoke, and to let the oppressed go free, and break every yoke? Is it not to divide your bread with the hungry, and bring the homeless poor into the house; when you see the naked, to cover him; and not to hide yourself from your own flesh? Then your light will break out like the dawn, and your recovery will speedily spring forth; and your righteousness will go before you; the glory of the Lord will be your rear guard. Then you will call, and the Lord will answer; you will cry, and He will say, 'Here I am.' If you remove the yoke from your midst, the pointing of the finger, and

speaking wickedness, And if you give yourself to the hungry, and satisfy the desire of the afflicted, then your light will rise in darkness, and your gloom will become like midday. And the Lord will continually guide you, and satisfy your desire in scorched places, and give strength to your bones; and you will be like a watered garden, and like a spring of water whose waters do not fail. And those from among you will rebuild the ancient ruins; you will raise up the age-old foundations; and you will be called the repairer of the breach, the restorer of the streets in which to dwell. If because of the Sabbath, you turn your foot from doing your own pleasure on My holy day, and call the Sabbath a delight, the holy day of the Lord honorable, and shall honor it, desisting from your own ways, from seeking your own pleasure, and speaking your own word, then you will take delight in the Lord, and I will make you ride on the heights of the earth; and I will feed you with the heritage of Jacob your father, for the mouth of the Lord has spoken. Behold, the Lord's hand is not so short that it cannot save; neither is His ear so dull that it cannot hear. But your iniquities have made a separation between you and your God, and your sins have hidden His face from you, so that He does not hear. For your hands are defiled with blood, and your fingers with iniquity; your lips have spoken falsehood, your tongue mutters wickedness. No one sues righteously and no one pleads honestly. They trust in confusion, and speak lies; they conceive mischief, and bring forth iniquity. They hatch adders' eggs and weave the spider's web; He who eats of their eggs dies, And from that which is crushed a snake breaks forth. Their webs will not become clothing, nor will they cover themselves with their works; their works are works of iniquity, and an act of violence is in their hands. Their feet run to evil, and they hasten to shed innocent blood; their thoughts are thoughts of iniquity; devastation and destruction are in their highways. They do not know the way of peace, and there is no justice in their tracks; they have made their paths crooked; whoever treads on them does not know peace. Isaiah 58:3-59:8

Fasting for the right reason

Fasting for the right reason is important. In college we had to fast for three days as a homework assignment. I felt no benefit in my spiritual life because there was no spiritual motivation in its activity. It was simply for a grade. There are plenty of people who fast in today's world. They fast to lose weight. They fast to be noticed by others and gain approval. In Scripture we see many passages that illustrate right reasons to fast: as a sign of true repentance, in order to seek the intervention of God in our circumstances, to know God more intimately, and to obtain the spiritual power needed to overcome the enemy. All of these can be accomplished through fasting.

Fasting in relationship with God

There are many in the Bible who fasted who didn't even have a personal relationship with God. Jesus pointed out that the Pharisees fasted twice a week, yet they didn't even recognize that He was God's son. Their fasting was void of any relationship with Him. You will find if you want to go deeper in this area, that it is only through relationship and dependence on God that you can truly fast. You must frequently tap into the strength of the Vine in order to resist the fleeting rush of physical nutrition.

Fasting by the Spirit's leading and direction

I had a new experience in 2004. I had been studying about Jesus' temptation in the wilderness and noted that He had arrived there through the Spirit's leading. So I told the Lord I would like to learn to fast at the Spirit's leading. After all, when Jesus entered the wilderness, He didn't know that He would be fasting for forty days. He simply obeyed the Holy Spirit who told Him when not to eat, and when to eat. So on this particular occasion, I asked the Lord to tell me when to start and when to stop fasting. I felt a strong impression to begin the fast in my quiet time, one morning. But I didn't have a clue how long a fast it would be, or how I would know it was to be over. Day one and two went by. On the morning of day three, I noticed that there was a women's potluck at our church that evening. I simply hadn't noticed it until that morning.

But now I wondered if I should break my fast? Should I continue it? So I simply prayed, "Lord, You know how long you want me to continue. When You're ready for me to stop, just make it clear."

That night I spent some time praying at the church before the event but didn't see or hear anyone until ten minutes before the scheduled time for the event to begin. There had been a sign up sheet for those who wanted to come, but I hadn't signed up, and I soon found out three others hadn't signed up either. Unbeknownst to us, the event had been cancelled, and all the ladies who had signed up had been called, but there were four ladies that night that the Lord had selected for a special blessing. He had planned His own potluck for us. Between us we had fried chicken, two salads and a dessert. (I had brought food to share even though I hadn't planned on eating.) I decided to end my fast and we had our own little intimate time of fellowship. We enjoyed a banquet of sharing, praising and goodies on the office worktable.

I felt that the Lord was saying at that moment that it was time to eat, not to fast. When I went home that night, I marveled at how the Lord had brought the four of us together so personally and at how distinctly He had showed me when to end the fast. It was a great experience, and in the days to follow I reaped a huge harvest of blessings as a result of that fast. Our family enjoyed more peace, ministries smacked of more power, and prayer doors were opened. It was a wonderful opportunity and it made me look forward to the next opportunity of fasting/feasting in the Spirit.

Here is a verse the Lord used to encourage me to continue in the middle of a fast: *He has filled the hungry with good things. Luke 1:53a*

It is difficult to even write about fasting. It is such a private encounter and Jesus spoke so strongly about not blowing the trumpets about acts of private devotion. But I feel the need to help people grow makes it important enough to share such personal encounters. If one person who does not understand the impact and benefit of fasting learns from this book and becomes a warrior of intercession, it will have monumental results and be worth it.

And whenever you fast, do not put on a gloomy face as the hypocrites do, for they neglect their appearance in order to be seen fasting by men. Truly I say to you, they have their reward in full. But you, when you fast, anoint your head, and wash your face so that you may not be seen fasting by men, but by your Father who is in secret; and your Father who sees in secret will repay you. Matthew 6:16-18

Jesus understood some things that the disciples didn't understand. While they were grocery shopping, he was feeding on a spiritual encounter with the woman at the well. While they were discussing the fact that they had forgotten to bring supplies for lunch, He was savoring peace. But how did He learn it? I believe He had to learn about fasting just like we do. He was tempted in all ways, like we are, and He was fully man as well as fully God. So, he had to learn about fasting through a process. When He fasted in the wilderness for forty days, I can't believe it was His first time. Through obedience, His Father led Him to learn how to fast.

And it's through a journey that we learn too. We have to come up against some situations, as tough as the demons the disciples faced,[7] to realize we need the power that only fasting provides. This thought has crossed my mind at times during fasting. Who knows? There might be something that crosses my path today that I will have the opportunity to rebuke or bind. My fasting will determine the outcome of the situation.

When you keep hitting the same wall, fasting may be the answer. We read in Judges chapter twenty:
Then all the sons of Israel and all the people went up and came to Bethel and wept; thus they remained there before the Lord and fasted that day until evening. And they offered burnt offerings and peace offerings before the Lord. And the sons of Israel inquired of the Lord (for the ark of the covenant of God was there in those days, and Phinehas the son of Eleazar, Aaron's son, stood before it to minister in those days), saying, "Shall I yet again go out to battle against the sons of my brother Benjamin, or shall I cease?" And the Lord said, "Go up, for tomorrow I will deliver them into your hand." So Israel

set men in ambush around Gibeah. And the sons of Israel went up against the sons of Benjamin on the third day and arrayed themselves against Gibeah, as at other times. Judges 20:26-30 So all of Benjamin who fell that day were 25,000 men who draw the sword; all these were valiant warriors. Judges 20:46

There are times when only fasting brings victory. Here is one example:

In December of 2001 our church had an important school board meeting. The board members were under tremendous financial burdens as a result of building new facilities. They shared with our school administrator that the school could not depend on any financial assistance from the church for student tuitions. In other words, the school would need ten more students to balance the budget; otherwise, the church might have to consider closing the school. Our administrator left the meeting shaken, but she and her assistant began to pray. The Lord gave each of them the same verse as they prayed: Matthew 17:20 "If you have faith as a mustard seed, you will say to this mountain, 'Move from here to there' and it will move, and nothing will be impossible for you." Here is her description of what took place:

We both saw and heard that our faith was not the size of a mustard seed but actually the size of a watermelon. For whatever reason, God used this picture to encourage us and as a reminder of what He was going to do. When I went into work the next day there was a watermelon on my desk. Mandy, our assistant administrator, and I have a special love for watermelons now.

We knew that the reality of the school growing to its needed capacity was nothing over which we had control. It was a huge mountain. To stay afloat we needed ten new students. Well, the Lord led me back to Matthew 17:20 and most importantly to Matthew 17:21 "However, this kind of faith does not go out except by prayer and fasting." So I challenged the staff that we needed to begin taking one day a week to fast and pray together during the hours of the school. It was a great time of fellowship and unity for the staff.

I believe that God would have worked no matter what we did, yet He allowed us to experience something so much deeper than I can even express. It was obvious He was at work because through our efforts there would be no way we could bring ten more students in one month.

During this time we did not advertise, we did not even express that there was a need for additional students. We only took our requests before God. It was only God who could bring in seventeen students like He did! It was as if He had taken His signet ring and placed it on the seal of the school.

In the area of fasting we will have to rely on the Holy Spirit to lead us. We are often unaware of what He is accomplishing as we do it.[8] Jake Deshazer, a member of Doolittle's Raiders, fasted for forty days while still in Japan. He told my Uncle Dick and Aunt Dorothy Mack that he didn't even know why he should be fasting for such a long time, but on the thirty-ninth day, Mitano Fuchida, who led the raid on Pearl Harbor, came to Jake and asked how to become a Christian.

What new things does God want to reveal to you through fasting. Start the adventure. Begin with a small commitment and allow the Lord to enlarge it. Don't let the failures of the past harass your new journey. Let the Lord be your tour guide and begin this new adventure!

Chapter 13 - Fight for Your Country

"History belongs to the intercessor..." Walter Wink

...Who gave Himself for our sins, that He might deliver us out of this present evil age, according to the will of our God and Father. Galatians 1:4

The first thing to do in getting our society back is to acknowledge the reality of where it is spiritually. I can think of no other passage which accurately accesses where America is right now than the following one.

For even though they knew God, they did not honor Him as God, or give thanks; but they became futile in their speculations, and their foolish heart was darkened. Professing to be wise, they became fools, and exchanged the glory of the incorruptible God for an image in the form of corruptible man and of birds and four-footed animals and crawling creatures. Therefore God gave them over in the lusts of their hearts to impurity, that their bodies might be dishonored among them. For they exchanged the truth of God for a lie, and worshiped and served the creature rather than the Creator, who is blessed forever. Amen. For this reason God gave them over to degrading passions; for their women exchanged the natural function for that which is unnatural, and in the same way also the men abandoned the natural function of the woman and burned in their desire toward one another, men with men committing indecent acts and receiving in their own persons the due penalty of their error. And just as they did not see fit to acknowledge God any longer, God gave them over to a depraved mind, to do those things which are not proper, being filled with all unrighteousness, wickedness, greed, evil; full of envy, murder, strife, deceit, malice; they are gossips, slanderers, haters of God, insolent, arrogant, boastful, inventors of evil, disobedient to parents, without understanding, untrustworthy, unloving, unmerciful; and, although they know the ordinance of God, that those who practice such things are worthy of death, they not only do the same, but also give hearty approval to those who practice them. Romans 1:21-32

We know God, but we do not honor Him. In this country, we have been allowing our legislators and judges to remove all references to God, the Ten Commandments and prayer from public places,

We have been blessed by God, but we do not thank Him. I recently visited Disneyland with some extended family members. We had boycotted them for six years as a result of their policy of allowing gay and lesbian days at the park, but I felt the Lord had given permission to spend time there with what extended family I have left and to invest in their spiritual development. (The fact that the trip was a gift also helped in the decision making process.) We attended a presentation in which Whoopi Goldberg represented a make-believe character called Califa throughout depictions of California's history, we saw Califa step in to save the day. i.e. a miner ready to give up, but because Califa says to keep going, he strikes it rich. Even though the history briefly touched on the missions throughout California, and even showed the priests asking for God's blessing on this land, nowhere does Disney acknowledge that the source for California's blessings is God. This is just one example of how man takes credit, even in fun, for the gratitude only God should receive. I joked with family members as we left the presentation, "God will be happy to know that Califa deserves all the credit for making California as prosperous and blessed as it is today."

Thus, we become darkened in our understanding. When we do not honor and thank God, our minds are darkened. We find ourselves going in mental circles, because God is wisdom. Without Him, there is little knowledge or progress.

We worship the things God has made, not the One who has made them. We can see people all around us worshiping the earth, the sun, animals, trees, cars, bodies, pleasure and much more. Everything from a spotted owl to a kangaroo rat is worthy of time and attention, except the One who created them all.

There is an abandoning of the pure and right for the degrading. As the mind becomes darkened it is no longer able to discern right from wrong. A spiritual deadness takes over and evil begins to look good. Good begins to look evil. Satan is the father of lies and once he gets us on his train, we are headed for a destination of deceit.

We reap the fruits of sin: greed, boastfulness, untrustworthiness, disobedience, etc. Employers now report they cannot find good workers. We see that when our minds are given over to unfruitful things, we become untrustworthy. Parents are having a hard time raising children. The choices of our society to allow rude and disrespectful behavior and to promote it in the media results in an atmosphere of rebellion, and this bears fruit in the lives of our children. Greed and boastfulness identify the state of our people, not humility and thriftiness, as in many former generations.

We give approval to others who practice these things. Blatant encouragement of homosexual activity is broadcast throughout our world. Some give agreement just by their silence and inaction. Remember Saul gave agreement just by holding the coats of others as Stephen was stoned.[9]

Just as these are steps to decay for a country, so they can also be the road map to restoration. The first thing we must do in getting our country back is to acknowledge our sin. Use the list above in your prayer time and pray corporate as well as personal confessions over these items. Then begin to incorporate the opposite into your every day living:

Honor God. Honor Him through His own decreed methods. He loves it when we honor Him through the tithe. He feels loved when we set aside our own activities and honor Him on the Sabbath, not a set of rules, but a heart attitude. He feels loved when we trust His Word over our own. He loves it when we honor him before other men and when we do not shrink back from speaking His name in public arenas. *I will always obey Your law, forever and ever. I will walk about in freedom, for I have sought out Your precepts. I will speak of Your statutes before kings and will not be put to shame for I delight in Your commands because I love them. Psalm 119:44-46*

(NIV) And whatever you ask in My name, that will I do, that the Father may be glorified in the Son. If you ask Me anything in My name, I will do it. John 14:13-14 ...that whatever you ask of the Father in My name, He may give to you. John 15:16b And in that day you will ask Me no question. Truly, truly, I say to you, if you shall ask the Father for anything, He will give it to you in My name. Until now you have asked for nothing in My name; ask, and you will receive, that your joy may be made full. John 16:23-24

Thank God for His care. Joyfully acknowledge each meal and each blessing as coming from His hand. Use every opportunity to thank Him for His intervention into your life. Thank Him more than you ask Him for things. Begin and end each prayer with praise and thanksgiving.

As you do this you will see Him open your understanding on any issue. He did this for Daniel. We read that He gave Daniel the ability to understand difficult problems. Francis A. Schaeffer, in the book How Should We Then Live,[10] discusses how advances in every area of art, science, literature, etc. were made at the end of the Dark Ages as people sought to honor God through their work, i.e. Handel's music, Galileo's scientific findings, Michelangelo's sculptures.

Worship the Creator over His creation. Use each opportunity of discovery in God's World to pause and worship His wisdom and power. (i.e. When you find out mind-boggling things about honey bees or orchids, stop and offer praise to the One who created them.)

Cling to the pure and upright. Avoid all hints of sin and deceitfulness. Put away any known sin and all doubtful habits.

Look for and promote the fruits of righteousness (Galatians 5:22). As you do these things, you will see the Fruit of the Spirit developed in your life and family.

Only give approval to things that are pure and right. Be careful here. Approval can be given to wrong things simply by silence or no action.

And He saw that there was no man, and was astonished that there was no one to intercede; then His own arm brought salvation to Him; and His righteousness upheld Him. Isaiah 59:16

Today, don't let God be astonished that there are few who intercede for your country. Let Him be surprised by your consistent and purposeful intercession. Like a sentry on duty, walk around the needs of your country and point them out to the Heavenly Commander and Chief.

If I shut up the heavens so that there is no rain, or if I command the locust to devour the land, or if I send pestilence among My people, and My people who are called by My name humble themselves and pray, and seek My face and turn from their wicked ways, then I will hear from heaven, will forgive their sin, and will heal their land. 2 Chronicles 7:13-14

And for this reason God will send upon them a deluding influence so that they might believe what is false, in order that they all may be judged who did not believe the truth, but took pleasure in wickedness. 2 Thessalonians 2:12

Prayer journal entry:

6/26/02 Started praying over Pledge of Allegiance controversy. The words "under God" may be stricken from it in court proceedings.

3/04 The court has declared the words will stay for now.

3/04 Judge in San Francisco began issuing gay marriage licenses.

8/04 California Supreme Court ruled that these were illegal.

In the summer of 2003 we visited Ralph and Pam Neighbor who pastor a church in Chino, California. Ralph shared with us on that visit that recently the City Council had said that they would no longer allow him to pray at their meetings "in the name of Jesus." Ralph replied that if he could not pray in the name of Jesus that his prayers would not be effective. He shared with them that everything

God grants believers comes through the mighty name of Jesus. This immediately went on my prayer list. Month after month I brought this set of circumstances up to the Lord.

A year later I was talking to a friend who attends another church in that city. She shared that shortly after the City Council had made this mandate, her church had gotten T-shirts made up that said, "We pray in the name of Jesus!," and that they wore them all over town. It wasn't long before the council reversed its earlier motion. Praise the Lord!

The enemy wants to make you believe that one little person can't make a difference in the events of a nation. But we know from the life of David that it only took one to fling a stone than changed the course of events for the nation Israel. One boy, Josiah, got his country back in the Word. One preacher, Peter, preached a sermon that won thousands. One prophet, Samuel, was listening when God was ready to speak. And you too can make a difference every day through your prayers of faith.

But I will camp around My house because of an army, Because of him who passes by and returns; and no oppressor will pass over them anymore, for now I have seen with My eyes. Zechariah 9:8

First of all, then, I urge that entreaties and prayers, petitions and thanksgivings, be made on behalf of all men, for kings and all who are in authority, in order that we may lead a tranquil and quiet life in all godliness and dignity. This is good and acceptable in the sight of God our Savior, who desires all men to be saved and to come to the knowledge of the truth. 1 Timothy 2:1-4

Not long ago I met a woman named Linda, who has taken this challenge seriously. Several years ago Linda felt God calling her to intercede full time for her country. She sold her condominium and all her treasures and moved to Washington DC where she volunteers at the Pentagon. All day long as she guides visitors around, her real purpose is to pray for her country. It was interesting to hear how the

Lord has provided for her ministry. Linda loves to entertain and has had missionaries and diplomats from all over the world at her dinner parties. One of her biggest sacrifices came when she offered the Lord all her dishes, as well as everything else, in order to be obedient to His call. She left her home, decorated with tulips, which she loves, and thrust herself into the hands of the Almighty. God answered by giving her a place to live, almost for free, decorated with gorgeous tulips and completely furnished with lots of space and a supply of beautiful dishes on which to serve her prayer-backed cuisine.

Linda shared with us something that I don't think many people know. She told us that on the National Day of Prayer, the Word of God is continually read out loud by different people right near the steps of the Capitol building. She has had the privilege of being one of the readers.

There is much spiritual activity that takes place every day in and around our nation's capitol. You may not be able to get on a plane today, but you can turn aside and spend some time with the One whose arms reach around the entire world. Ask Him today to open eyes and hearts to spiritual truth. Plead with Him to honor the devotion of our forefathers and to pour out His Spirit and bring re-vival. God may not be asking you to give up your job or your home in order to save your country, but I know He is asking for more of your time and attention. After all, America is a great country. It is worth the trouble of spiritual warfare.

Recently, my husband and our friend, Dr. Marshall Foster,[11] did a special Independence Day message together. They reminded us of the sacrifices of the founding fathers who trusted God with their lives, their fortunes and their sacred honor. How can we offer the Lord any less? The peace and freedom we enjoy today was bought with a high price. It cost many of them their very lives. Today, become a true patriot! Intercede for your country. Acknowledge its sins. Press God for His miraculous work of revival. You too may find your name in future history books. But if not, you will be registered in God's book of intercessors. He saves each tear we shed and our prayers are the incense of His dwelling place.

We must acknowledge the sins of our country

Abortion

So innocent blood will not be shed in the midst of your land which the Lord your God gives you as an inheritance, and blood guiltiness be on you. Deuteronomy 19:10

Moreover, Manasseh shed very much innocent blood until he had filled Jerusalem from one end to another; besides his sin with which he made Judah sin, in doing evil in the sight of the Lord. 2 Kings 21:16

Thus I shall judge you, like women who commit adultery or shed blood are judged; and I shall bring on you the blood of wrath and jealousy. Ezekiel 16:38 And you shall say, "Thus says the Lord God," a city shedding blood in her midst, so that her time will come. Ezekiel 22:3a

You have become guilty by the blood which you have shed. Ezekiel 22:4a

And shed innocent blood, the blood of their sons and their daughters, whom they sacrificed to the idols of Canaan; and the land was polluted with the blood. Psalm 106:38

Haughty eyes, a lying tongue, and hands that shed innocent blood. Proverbs 6:17

Their feet run to evil, and they hasten to shed innocent blood; their thoughts are thoughts of iniquity, devastation and destruction are in their highways. Isaiah 59:7

If you do not oppress the alien, the orphan, or the widow, and do not shed innocent blood in this place, nor walk after other gods to your own ruin, Jeremiah 7:6

Thus says the Lord, "Do justice and righteousness, and deliver the one who has been robbed from the power of his oppressor. Also do not mistreat or do violence to the stranger, the orphan, or the widow; and do not shed innocent blood in this place." Jeremiah 22:3

Egypt will become a waste, and Edom will become a desolate wilderness, Because of the violence done to the sons of Judah, in whose land they have shed innocent blood. Joel 3:19

The sin of Judah is written down with an iron stylus; with a diamond point it is engraved upon the tablet of their heart, and on the horns of their altars, as they remember their children. Jeremiah 17:1-2

Forsaking the Lord

Know therefore and see that it is evil and bitter for you to forsake the Lord your God, and the dread of Me is not in you," declares the Lord God of hosts. Jeremiah 2:19b We have become like those over whom Thou hast never ruled, like those who were not called by Thy name. Isaiah 63:19 I permitted Myself to be sought by those who did not ask for Me; I permitted Myself to be found by those who did not seek Me. I said, "Here am I, here am I," to a nation which did not call on My name. "I have spread out My hands all day long to a rebellious people, who walk in the way which is not good, following their own thoughts, a people who continually provoke Me to My face, offering sacrifices in gardens and burning incense on bricks." Isaiah 65:1-3 "And you shall say to them, 'This is the nation that did not obey the voice of the Lord their God or accept correction; truth has perished and has been cut off from their mouth.'" Jeremiah 7:28

Belittling the Word of the Lord

"Behold, days are coming," declares the Lord God, "When I will send a famine on the land, not a famine for bread or a thirst for water, but rather for hearing the words of the Lord." Amos 8:11

We must turn from our sin

For if you truly amend your ways and your deeds, if you truly practice justice between a man and his neighbor, if you do not oppress the alien, the orphan, or the widow, and do not shed innocent blood in this place, nor walk after other gods to your own ruin, then I will let you dwell in this place, in the land that I gave to your fathers forever and ever. Jeremiah 7:5-7

I now rejoice, not that you were made sorrowful, but that you were made sorrowful to the point of repentance; for you were made sorrowful according to the will of God, so that you might not suffer loss in anything through us. For the sorrow that is according to the will of God produces a repentance without regret, leading to salvation, but the sorrow of the world produces death. For behold what earnestness this very thing, this godly sorrow, has produced in you: what vindication of yourselves, what indignation, what fear, what longing, what zeal, what avenging of wrong! 2 Corinthians 7:9-11a

We must plead for mercy

On your walls, O Jerusalem, I have appointed watchmen; all day and all night they will never keep silent. You who remind the Lord, take no rest for yourselves; and give Him no rest until He establishes and makes Jerusalem a praise in the earth. Isaiah 62:6-7

We must cry out for repentance

Get yourself up on a high mountain, O Zion, bearer of good news, lift up your voice mightily, O Jerusalem, bearer of good news; lift it up, do not fear. Say to the cities of Judah, "Here is your God!" Isaiah 40:9

Cry loudly, do not hold back; raise your voice like a trumpet, and declare to My people their transgression, and to the house of Jacob their sins. Isaiah 58:1

God may or may not relent

"If that nation against which I have spoken turns from its evil, I will relent concerning the calamity I planned to bring on it. Or at another moment I might speak concerning a nation or concerning a kingdom to build up or to plant it; if it does evil in My sight by not obeying My voice, then I will think better of the good with which I had promised to bless it." Jeremiah 18:8-10

"I have hidden My face from this city because of all their wickedness: 'Behold, I will bring to it health and healing, and I will heal them; and I will reveal to them an abundance of peace and truth.'" Jeremiah 33:5B-6

For the iniquity of the daughter of my people is greater than the sin of Sodom, which was overthrown as in a moment, and no hands were turned toward her. Lamentations 4:6

Then the word of the Lord came to me saying, "Son of man, if a country sins against Me by committing unfaithfulness, and I stretch out My hand against it, destroy its supply of bread, send famine against it, and cut off from it both man and beast, even though these three men, Noah, Daniel, and Job were in its midst, by their own righteousness they could only deliver themselves," declares the Lord God. "If I were to cause wild beasts to pass through the land, and they depopulated it, and it became desolate so that no one would pass through it because of the beasts, though these three men were in its midst, as I live," declares the Lord God, "They could not deliver either their sons or their daughters. They alone would be delivered, but the country would be desolate. Or if I should bring a sword on that country and say, 'Let the sword pass through the country and cut off man and beast from it,' even though these three men were in its midst, as I live," declares the Lord God, "they could not deliver either their sons or their daughters, but they alone would be delivered. Or if I should send a plague against that country and pour out My wrath in blood on it, to cut off man and beast from it, even though Noah, Daniel, and Job were in its midst, as I live," declares the Lord God, "They could not deliver either their son or their daughter. They would deliver only themselves by their righteousness." For thus says the Lord God, "How much more when I send My four severe judgments against Jerusalem: sword, famine, wild beasts, and plague to cut off man and beast from it!" Yet, behold, survivors will be left in it who will be brought out, both sons and daughters. Behold, they are going to come forth to you and you will see their conduct and actions; then you will be comforted for the calamity which I have brought against Jerusalem for everything which I have brought upon it. Then they will comfort you when you see their conduct and actions, for you will know that I have not done in vain whatever I did to it," declares the Lord God. Ezekiel 14:12-23

God's judgment isn't always seen through invasion. God can make our wise men officials and rulers like drunks in a sleepy state. A foolish nation reaps its own punishment and no other nation even needs to help out.

"And I shall make her princes and her wise men drunk, her governors, her prefects, and her mighty men, that they may sleep a perpetual sleep and not wake up," declares the King, whose name if the Lord of hosts. Jeremiah 51:57

Remember that judgment is not a sign of abandonment

For neither Israel nor Judah has been forsaken by his God, the Lord of hosts, although their land is full of guilt Before the Holy One of Israel. Jeremiah 51:5

What we must do for revival to take place:

Ask

Ask rain from the Lord at the time of the spring rain— The Lord who makes the storm clouds; and He will give them showers of rain, vegetation in the field to each man. Zechariah 10:1 "For I am the Lord their God, and I will answer them." Zechariah 10:6b

Prepare

Open your doors, O Lebanon, that a fire may feed on your cedars. Zechariah 11:1

When the news of the judgment pronounced against Judge Roy Moore, for posting the Ten Commandments in his court was publicized, we took comfort in these verses: *He it is who reduces rulers to nothing, who makes the judges of the earth meaningless. Isaiah 40:23 Whatever you devise against the Lord, He will make a complete end of it. Distress will not rise up twice. Nahum 1:9 There is no wisdom and no understanding and no counsel against the Lord. Proverbs 21:30*

My husband has done more than just pray for his country. He writes articles in our local newspaper, calling attention to truth and the words of Scripture as they pertain to the issues of our day. His efforts may seem to some like a finger in a leaky dam, but when he stands before the Lord, he will know that he has done what he could to restore a nation of greatness to its roots of godliness.

My friend Galen has organized people to pray for every principal, vice-principal and career counselor in our entire Corona-Norco Unified School District, as well as federal, state and local elected officials. He also has written a course entitled, "Active Faith," which teaches Christians to apply the Word of God in current life issues. Galen and his wife, Kathy, travel to other churches training Christians to enter the arena of making a difference.

Another friend, Joyce Smith, has organized the churches in the area of Lake Elsinore, to pray together regularly, and has held community-wide events calling for revival.[12] It all began just by Joyce walking the streets of her city and praying. Then she began praying with others from different churches. Then the Lord impressed on them to work together to distribute copies of the Jesus Video to every home in Lake Elsinore. They had no budget but as they obeyed, the Lord provided $80,000 for this project to be completed.[13] Now Joyce works as the area coordinator for the National Day of Prayer.

You don't have to be wise, well trained, rich, or educated to fight in this war. God is not looking for the clever or even the persuasive to do battle on this field. He is looking for those who are willing to acknowledge that they are weak and dependant. He is searching for the willing and the faithful. He is simply asking us to show up and allow Him to work.

Turn the hearts of the fathers back to the children, and the disobedient to the attitude of the righteous; so as to make ready a people prepared for the Lord. Luke 1:17b

God is not opposed to employing thousands of His people to fight His war, but most of the time He finds the majority of them unusable. [20]

Chapter 14 - Put on the Dancing Shoes of Praise

We can enjoy the power of praise in the most discouraging of circumstances. God is the God of the Impossible and He can turn any situation around. This is what allows us to put on our dancing shoes when others are moping and whining.

Daniel and Israel were in big trouble. The nation was a pile of physical, emotional and spiritual rubble. They were taken as captives to a spiritually decadent country. God's people had been totally humiliated before their enemies. They now lived among and served idol worshippers.

As we look into the writings of the Minor Prophets we see that for years God had been warning them. He kept pleading with His people to turn from idol worship which meant put anything before Him. Over and over He had sent messages, through the prophets, that were blatant object lessons, so that they would have their hearts softened and change their ways. But these reminders and warnings were rejected by people who didn't want to hear them. They were listening to prophets, but only to the ones who were saying things they wanted to hear.

So a time of judgment came and God allowed His people to suffer the consequences of their actions. They reached out for the old familiar spiritual strength and resources of God in the battle, but there was no response. They were left with human ideas and strength and found that they were easily conquered.

God's people were taken captive. They were no longer free as God intended for them to be. They were not the conquerors, but the conquered. And they were being led away in chains from the land and blessings that were promised to them.

But in the midst of it all this trouble and pain and sorrow, God opened a window of hope through the prayer life of Daniel. Three times a day Daniel ran to God: He lived in a place where hope flourished. Praise is hope spoken out loud, and it became a language that Daniel was fluent in speaking.

- He dreamed God-dreams for his people in the midst of their misery.
- He asked God to work in the midst of spiritual decadence.
- He listened to God's thoughts instead of to his own discouragement.
- He flourished in the heavenly realm, even though he was in earthly bondage.

Daniel chose to hunker down in God. *The Lord is good, a stronghold in the day of trouble, and He knows those who take refuge in Him. Nahum 1:7* The Lord knows in the middle of your trouble if you are hiding in Him, or somewhere else.

Troubles make us grow, so we can't be sheltered from them, but we can be sheltered in them. Where are you in your troubles? Are you enjoying the comfort and refuge of the stronghold?

Here's a promise to hold on to:
Blessed are you who weep now, for you shall laugh. Luke 6:21b

Blessing follows obedience, and we see that God chose to give Daniel three wonderful gifts as a result of his spiritual hunger for righteousness. What did God give Daniel?

1. Favor and compassion with his captors
Now God granted Daniel favor and compassion in the sight of the commander of the officials. Daniel 1:19 Had he at some time requested this in prayer?

2. Knowledge and wisdom in every area
God gave them knowledge and intelligence in every branch of literature and wisdom. Daniel 1:17b Had Daniel asked for this?

3. The ability to solve difficult problems

"This was because an extraordinary spirit, knowledge and insight, interpretation of dreams, explanation of enigmas, and solving of difficult problems were found in this Daniel, whom the king named Belteshazzar. Let Daniel now be summoned, and he will declare the interpretation." Daniel 5:12

"But I personally have heard about you, that you are able to give interpretations and solve difficult problems. Now if you are able to read the inscription and make its interpretation known to me, you will be clothed with purple and wear a necklace of gold around your neck, and you will have authority as the third ruler in the kingdom." Daniel 5:16

In reference to solving difficult problems: Why did God allow David to face a lion and a bear? So that when He faced a giant, he would have the experience of knowing that the Almighty, powerful God could help him. Why did God allow a challenge for Daniel and his friends over the issue of food? He did it so that they would be prepared to stand up to a king who tried to put himself in God's place. That's why the Lord allows you and me to face little trials. They prepare us for bigger ones up ahead.

What gifts Daniel received from the Lord! Who wouldn't dance with these gifts? Do you realize that these are gifts the Lord wants to also give you? These are natural blessings that come to anyone in a connected relationship to the Almighty. Know this: God didn't give Daniel anything He wouldn't give you also.

Therefore, my brethren, you also were made to die to the Law through the body of Christ, that you might be joined to another, to Him who was raised from the dead, that we might bear fruit for God. Romans 7:4

The important thing about praise is to do it even before we see the results. God wants us to dance a dance of praise before we see the solution to our problems. We can do this if we place our thoughts on the character of God. He is faithful. He is trustworthy. Our toes begin to tap at the thought. Our problems may be mounting with a fury, but if we focus on who God is, our feet can't help but dance at the thought. He is mighty. He is victorious. The thoughts make us jump to our feet. In the midst of misery, slavery and doom we can begin to rise up and leap.

We, like Daniel, need to be reminded that God is...

Compassionate
Because He delights in unchanging love, He will again have compassion on us; He will tread our iniquities under foot. Yes, Thou will cast all their sins in to the depths of the sea. Micah 7:18b-19
The Lord is slow to anger and great in power, and the Lord will by no means leave the guilty unpunished. In whirlwind and storm is His way, and clouds are the dust beneath His feet. Nahum 1:3
For after all it is only just for God to repay with affliction those who afflict you, and to give relief to you who are afflicted and to us as well when the Lord Jesus shall be revealed from heaven with His mighty angels in flaming fire. 2 Thessalonians 1:6-7

Wise
The Lord by wisdom founded the earth; by understanding He established the heavens. By knowledge the deeps were broken up and the skies drip with dew. Proverbs 3:19

God is the source of all wisdom. Your understanding is limited when your connection to Him is limited.

A Revealer of Mysteries
...that their hearts may be encouraged, having been knit together in love, and attaining to all the wealth that comes from the full assurance of understanding, resulting in a true knowledge of God's mystery, that is, Christ Himself, in whom are hidden all the treasures of wisdom and knowledge. Colossians 2:2-3

Who cares what problems you face if the One who faces them with you understands all things and can help you solve difficult problems? When you are in the fire who is in there with you? When you spend the night in the lion's den who is camping next to you? When you're trying to bring a country through a famine, like Joseph, who is giving you your ideas? When you're in a difficult marriage, whose insights are you following? When you trust the Lord to pay the next bill, who is in charge of your finances?

Perhaps you are in the middle of some impossible circumstances yourself. Take heart in this: you can know God and be connected to His fountain of compassion, wisdom and understanding. He's the vine and you can be His branch. *"I am the vine, you are the branches; he who abides in Me, and I in him, he bears much fruit; for apart from Me you can do nothing. John 15:5.* He has all the good stuff and He chooses to send it through you.

What's your life like right now? Do you feel like a captive in a foreign land? Are you wondering why someone who doesn't love or honor God holds the keys to your shackles, or at least your paycheck?

God can change others' attitudes towards you. He can teach you what to do in any situation. He can solve your most difficult problems.

But those who seek the Lord understand all things. Proverbs 28:5b My son, if you will receive my sayings, and treasure my commandments within you, make your ear attentive to wisdom, incline your heart to understanding; for if you cry for discernment, lift your voice for understanding; for the Lord gives wisdom; from His mouth come knowledge and understanding. Proverbs 2:1-3

He stores up sound wisdom for the upright
He is a shield to those who walk in integrity, guarding the paths of justice, and He preserves the way of His godly ones. Then you will discern righteousness and justice and equity and every good course. For wisdom will enter your heart, and knowledge will be pleasant to your soul; discretion will guard you, understanding will watch over you. Proverbs 2:7-11
And He answered and said to them, "To you it has been granted to know the mysteries of the kingdom of heaven, but to them it has not

been granted." For whoever has, to him shall more be given, and he shall have an abundance; but whoever does not have, even what he has shall be taken away from him. Matthew 13:11-12

Doing wickedness is like sport to a fool; and so is wisdom to a man of understanding. Proverbs 10:23

We have a choice when trouble hits to put on the dancing shoes of praise in any situation. In Habakkuk, chapter three we see the prophet facing a bleak future head on with the mind and words of praise. It is the course of action he chose.

Then we see him choose the attitude of truly wanting God's will. It's the best possible way to pray! It comes from the most loving Father, who knows all things and cares deeply about us. We should embrace His will, not run from it. Why would I want my own way? I know nothing about the future. I change my mind like I change clothes. It doesn't matter how big my enemy is, if it's God's will, he's history! No one can override His decisions. No one can veto His purposes.

Thus says the Lord, though they are at full strength and likewise many, even so, they will be cut off and pass away. Nahum 1:12

Yet it was I who destroyed the Amorite before them, though his height was like the height of cedars and he was strong as the oaks; I even destroyed his fruit above and his root below. Amos 2:9

And all the inhabitants of the earth are accounted as nothing, But He does according to His will in the host of heaven and among the inhabitants of earth; and no one can ward off His hand or say to Him, 'What hast Thou done?' Daniel 4:35

We also see how Daniel began to access God's authority over every circumstance. If we take the following Scriptures to heart, we will begin to do the same.

In order that the living might know that the Most High God is ruler over the rest of mankind. Daniel 4:17b "All things have been handed over to Me by My Father, and no one knows who the Son is except the

Father, and who the Father is except the Son, and anyone to whom the Son wills to reveal Him." Luke 10:22 And having summoned His twelve disciples, He gave them authority over unclean spirits, to cast them out, and to heal every kind of disease and every kind of sickness. Matthew 10:1 And he said to him, "My child, you have always been with me, and all that is mine is yours." Luke 15:31

When we are in a vital, obedient relationship with God, there is nothing we cannot have authority over. If we are aligned with His will, there is no prayer request too high or difficult for Him

We have to live in the scary to know the magnificent. We would never have seen the mighty miracles found in the book of Daniel if he and his three friends had not faced life threatening circumstances. Daniel had to come up with the king's dream and its interpretation or face a death sentence. Shadrach, Meshach and Abed-nego, had to stand up to the king's decree or be killed in order to see God in the midst of a fire that didn't burn. And we see Daniel experiencing revelations in his dreams, so that he could receive understanding and see a nation restored.[14]

"There is not a man on earth who could declare the matter for the king. Moreover, the thing which the king demands is difficult, and there is no one else who could declare it to the king except gods, whose dwelling place is not with mortal flesh." Daniel 2:10b-11

Then Daniel went to his house and informed his friends, Hananiah, Mishael and Azariah, about the matter, in order that they might request compassion from the God of heaven concerning this mystery, [15] so that Daniel and his friends might not be destroyed with the rest of the wise men of Babylon. Then the mystery was revealed to Daniel in a night vision.[16] Then Daniel blessed the God of heaven; Daniel answered and said, "Let the name of God be blessed forever and ever, for wisdom and power belong to Him." And it is He who changes the times and the epochs; He removes kings and establishes kings; He gives wisdom to wise men, and knowledge to men of understanding." It is He who reveals the profound and hidden things;

He knows what is in the darkness, and the light dwells with Him. "To Thee, O God of my fathers, I give thanks and praise, for Thou hast given me wisdom and power; even now Thou hast made known to me what we requested of Thee, For Thou hast made known to us the king's matter." Daniel 2:17-23

And His disciples answered Him, "Where will anyone be able to find enough to satisfy these men with bread here in a desolate place?" Mark 8:4 But He said, "The things impossible with men are possible with God." Luke 18:27

Ruth Meyers tells us, in her book, <u>Thirty-One Days of Praise,</u>[17] that we can tune into God's presence through our praise. Life's circumstances can seem horribly out of sync, but our praise can tune our hearts up and invite the presence of the Almighty. She also says that we benefit more in our trials when we learn to praise God through them. I highly recommend her book and the method of using Scripture to praise the Lord each day.

When you find yourself in an impossible situation and you hear the voices of friends and acquaintances say things like, "It's too bad you believe in God, it's too bad he doesn't seem to care or help you right now." Put on your dancing shoes! Start praying! Start praising! Start asking for God's will! Start accessing the resources He puts within the reach of those who desire His will!

What is God's ultimate will in this situation?

The Prophet tells Hezekiah that the Lord has decreed his death. Hezekiah went to prayer in the face of what He believes was the clear will and Word of the Lord. But God's ultimate will was for Hezekiah to intercede to victory. Perhaps you have received some life-threatening word, which is discouraging to you. Maybe this is God's will for you. But, think of Hezekiah. Perhaps this is just an opportunity for fifteen more years of blessing. The account in 2 Kings 20 doesn't say that Hezekiah praised the Lord. In fact he wept bitterly and reminded the Lord of his obedient life-style. But many others in Scripture have used praise to bring their hearts and minds into victory long before their eyes viewed it in the physical realm.

But as for me, I will watch expectantly for the Lord; I will wait for the God of my salvation. My God will hear me. Do not rejoice over me, O my enemy. Though I fall I will rise; though I dwell in darkness, the Lord is a light for me. Micah 7:7 -8

Praise God for how you have seen Him work in the past

Only give heed to yourself and keep your soul diligently, lest you forget the things which your eyes have seen, and lest they depart from your heart all the days of your life; but make them known to your sons and your grandsons. Deuteronomy 4:9

If you should say in your heart, 'These nations are greater than I; how can I dispossess them?' You shall not be afraid of them; you shall well remember what the Lord your God did to Pharaoh and to all Egypt. Deuteronomy 7:17-18

There is no better way to get praising than to walk through the steps of God's faithfulness in the past. Has He ever let you down? One of my favorite things to notice in my prayer journal[18] is all the financial difficulties that God has gotten us through. Year after year I see times of crises: an unexpected bill, car repairs, etc. Yet each one bears a "Praise the Lord!" The Lord has taken care of all of them!

Just follow the Lord's care, like a path of bread crumbs,[19] and you'll end up delighting in His awesome care. Beginning dancers, or those with two left feet like myself, have trouble just getting their feet to move correctly. But advanced dancers can twirl, and dip in the grip of a gifted partner. The more we relax in God's hand and enjoy the journey, the more He will be able to accomplish in the trials. So, let go of your inhibitions and fears. Recognize the ability of your Partner to lead and relax in His hands.

Praise Him today for the help He will give tomorrow

For Sheol cannot thank Thee, death cannot praise Thee; those who go down to the pit cannot hope for Thy faithfulness. It is the living who give thanks to Thee, as I do today; a father tells his sons about Thy faithfulness. The Lord will surely save me; so we will play my songs on stringed instruments all the days of our life at the house of the Lord. Isaiah 38:18

God will help you if you are His child. We are told in Philippians chapter four that we are not to worry about anything, but that we are to pray about everything. So why not begin to praise Him now for the help that will surely come in your situation. Put on the dancing shoes of praise and kick up your heels.

Finally, brethren, whatever is true, whatever is honorable, whatever is right, whatever is pure, whatever is lovely, whatever is of good repute, if there is any excellence and if anything worthy of praise, let your mind dwell on these things. Philippians 4:8

Paul knows how to dance, even with his feet in stocks! Despite how hopeless your circumstances may be right now, let's join him! Praise the Lord!

I thank my God in all my remembrance of you, always offering prayer with joy in my every prayer for you all, in view of your participation in the gospel from the first day until now. For I am confident of this very thing, that He who began a good work in you will perfect it until the day of Christ Jesus. For it is only right for me to feel this way about you all, because I have you in my heart, since both in my imprisonment and in the defense and confirmation of the gospel, you all are partakers of grace with me. Philippians 1:3-7

Now I want you to know, brethren that my circumstances have turned out for the greater progress of the gospel. Philippians 1:12

For I know that this shall turn out for my deliverance through your prayers and the provision of the Spirit of Jesus Christ, according to my earnest expectation and hope, that I shall not be put to shame in anything, but that with all boldness, Christ shall even now, as always, be exalted in my body, whether by life or by death. For to me, to live is Christ, and to die is gain. Philippians 1:19-21

But even if I am being poured out as a drink offering upon the sacrifice and service of your faith, I rejoice and share my joy with you all. Philippians 2:17

Rejoice in the Lord always; again I will say, rejoice! Philippians 4:4

Conclusion:

The enemy wants to convince you that:

You are only one person standing against a huge tidal wave of spiritual activity.

Your prayers can't possibly make a difference.

Your time could be spent better in working, rather than in praying.

You have no authority to challenge what is happening around you.

You are foolish to believe in the power of God.

I pray that this book will encourage you to believe that:

It only takes one to make a difference.

Every prayer is heard and responded to by the Living God.

Prayer is our work. We were created for relationship with God. Prayer is just that.

Prayer-directed work is more effective mere toil.

God has granted us the authority and opportunity to change our circumstances.

There is no one in Scripture who ever wished they had not trusted the Lord.

I am fully convinced that if you will carve out more time in your day to spend in fellowship and conversation with the Most High God, He will respond by allowing you to experience a greater depth of intimacy. You will also see Him work in the requests you make known. You will log for yourself journals of answered prayer. As He fulfills His part of this relationship, please let me know how He works in your life. Let's rejoice together over His marvelous goodness.

Sharon Riddle
www.oliveleafpublications.com

Endnotes

1 John 5:5ff

2 John 9:3

3 Gene Way, John Comer ©2003 Thirsty Moon River Publishing, 50 Miles, Gene Way Designee (all Admin. by EMI Christian Music Publishing)

4 In Waiting at the Window, I used this term to describe when hearts aren't right with each other, even if there is no known sin,. i.e. There might be hurt or misunderstanding, but not unconfessed sin.

5 Some people can fast for extended periods; for others it is not medically wise. A medically trained person should be consulted on extended periods of fasting. It is important to keep the body supplied with fluids, especially in hot, dry climates. Those who cannot handle fasting without any nutrient can give up rich foods or desserts. Some may only be able to give up some desired activity. Bill Bright fasted for forty days on many occasions, but he did take nutrient supplements to keep up his energy for his busy schedule. He wrote extensively on fasting at the end of a long fast that it is wise to return to a regular diet slowly.

6 *While the meat was still between their teeth, before it was chewed, the anger of the Lord was kindled against the people, and the Lord struck the people with a very severe plague. Numbers 11:33*

7 *Then the disciples came to Jesus privately and said, "Why could we not drive it out?" And He said to them, "Because of the littleness of your faith; for truly I say to you, if you have faith the size of a mustard seed, you will say to this mountain, 'Move from here to there,' and it will move; and nothing will be impossible to you. But this kind does not go out except by prayer and fasting." Matthew 17:19-21*

8 Daniel was unaware that his twenty-one days of fasting had moved heavenly forces to conquer the demonic one. Daniel 10:13.

9 *And when they had driven him out of the city, they began stoning him, and the witnesses laid aside their robes at the feet of a young man named Saul. Acts 7:58*

10 Francis A. Schaeffer, How Should We then Live? Crossway Books, 1983

11 Marshall Foster is the founder of the Mayflower Institute.

12 Joyce has helped coordinate events such as the Wave of Worship for the churches in her area.

13 Each church took one freewill offering towards the cause.

14 *So I was left alone and saw this great vision; yet no strength was left in me, for my natural color turned to a deathly pallor, and I retained no strength. Daniel 10:8*

15 They had a prayer meeting!

16 His prayer request was answered.

17 <u>Thirty-One Days of Praise</u> by Ruth Meyers. ©1994 Multnomah Publishing, Inc.

18 I keep a list of all the requests I have given to the Lord in prayer along with the dates they were requested. I note the date when they were answered and if they were granted, I color them with a highlighter to make them stand out on the page. One of the greatest testimonies to the Lord's faithfulness is that five years of pages are full of color.

19 Remember the story of Hansel and Gretel? They followed bread crumbs to get home. If we look closely at the steps of God's care, we will reach our destination of praise.

20 K.P. Yohannan, <u>Reflecting His Image</u>, p. 8 Gospel for Asia ©1998.